Access to agreement

A CONSUMER STUDY OF MEDIATION IN FAMILY DISPUTES

Access to agreement

A CONSUMER STUDY OF MEDIATION IN FAMILY DISPUTES

Gwynn Davis
Marian Roberts

OPEN UNIVERSITY PRESS
MILTON KEYNES · PHILADELPHIA

Open University Press
Open University Educational Enterprises Limited
12 Cofferidge Close
Stony Stratford
Milton Keynes MK11 1BY

and
242 Cherry Street
Philadelphia, PA 19106, USA

First published 1988

British Library Cataloguing in Publication Data

Davis, Gwynn
    Access to agreement: a consumer study
    of mediation in family disputes.
    1. Marriage counselling
    I. Title   II. Roberts, Marian
    362.8'286

    ISBN 0-335-09840-1
    ISBN 0-335-09830-4 Pbk

Library of Congress Cataloging-in-Publication Data

    Access to agreement: a consumer study of
mediation in family disputes/by Gwynn Davis and
Marian Roberts.
        p.   cm.
    Bibliography: p.
    Includes index.
    1. Family mediation – Great Britain – Case studies.
2. Marriage counseling – Great Britain – Case studies.
I. Roberts, Marian, II. Title.
HQ10.5.G7D36   988   362.8'286 – dc19   88-10209
ISBN 0-335-09840-1
ISBN 0-335-09830-4 (pbk)

Typeset by Rowland Phototypesetting Limited
Bury St Edmunds, Suffolk
Printed in Great Britain by Oxford University Press

Contents

Preface

This book is based on research undertaken at the South-East London (Bromley) Conciliation Bureau. We relied throughout on the support of the mediators, and of the administrative and secretarial staff at Bromley. It cannot be easy to allow other people to monitor one's work, but we would never have guessed this from the response of the bureau staff. We owe a special debt to Fred Gibbons, Co-ordinator of the bureau, for his friendliness and courtesy and for his quite remarkable lack of defensiveness in permitting us to research, in whatever way we wished, the project he devised.

Secondly, we are indebted to those parents who agreed to talk to us about their experience of family mediation. As far as we were concerned, their frankness and generosity were beyond price.

The research was financed, in large part, by the Nuffield Foundation who have given Gwynn Davis generous financial backing over some ten years. We are particularly grateful to Pat Thomas, Deputy Director of Nuffield, for her unstinting support. We were also fortunate to receive an additional research grant from the Worshipful Company of Weavers.

viii *Access to agreement*

The manuscript was typed by Kay Bader, who was also a valued colleague in other aspects of the 'Conciliation in Divorce' research study. Kay took on this secretarial task in the midst of an already busy researching life; she accepted with good humour all the additional demands that co-authorship can bring.

Finally, both authors wish to acknowledge the enormous debt which they owe to Simon Roberts. Simon contributed several key ideas which helped transform the manuscript from its original modest beginnings as a research report; he was, throughout the project, an unfailing source of encouragement and wise counsel.

PART 1

The idea

1

Introduction

This is a study of family mediation, centred on the work of a single agency, the South-East London (Bromley) Family Conciliation Bureau. The Bromley bureau was one of the first services set up in Britain in order to help with the resolution of disputes arising from the breakdown of a marriage or marriage-type relationship. The disputes that are brought to the attention of the bureau mainly concern children, but occasionally issues relating to the divorce suit, maintenance and property are also dealt with.

What is distinctive about this study is that its perspective is primarily that of the consumers, the parties to the dispute. These parents describe in their own words their experience of mediation as practised at Bromley. All the literature in this country looks at the subject from the standpoint either of the practitioner (Parkinson, 1986) or the academic (Davis, 1983 and 1983a, Dingwall, 1986, and Roberts, 1983). This is the first attempt to canvass the views of those who actually experience mediation and are the recipients of its supposed benefits. Our intention is to spotlight not only the goals and practices of one mediation agency, but also to shed light on a range of issues associated with the recent rapid and not uncontroversial rise of mediation as a way of responding to family disputes.

To begin it is necessary to set the introduction of family mediation in this country in a broader context. It is said that the modern conciliation movement began in 1913 in Cleveland, Ohio, where a conciliation branch of the municipal court was set up in order to assist litigants who were unable to obtain lawyers to settle their small claims. Participation in this procedure was voluntary; the judge acted as mediator and the outcome rested upon the consent of the parties (Auerbach, 1983, p. 97).

However, it is over the past two decades that a rapid growth of extra-legal dispute-resolution agencies has taken place in the West, particularly in the USA. These schemes range from grassroots initiatives to government-sponsored projects incorporated within the judicial system as substitutes for formal adjudication.

Enthusiasm for these extra-legal forms – mediation and arbitration in the main – is of very recent origin in this country and is perhaps only now at a level comparable to that experienced in North America a decade ago. The one exception, in the sense of there having been an alternative dispute-resolution model of long standing, is in the field of industrial relations, where as early as 1896 (The Conciliation Act) and 1919 (The Industrial Courts Act) provision was made for the appropriate minister to make arrangements for the settlement of trade disputes by conciliation or arbitration. The Employment Protection Act 1975 repealed the Conciliation Act 1896 and parts of the Industrial Courts Act 1919 and set up the Advisory, Conciliation and Arbitration Service (ACAS) in order 'to help employers, workers and their union representatives resolve trade disputes and improve the conduct of their industrial relations'.[1]

The first family mediation agency, the Bristol Courts Family Conciliation Service (BCFCS), was set up in 1978, followed by the Bromley bureau in 1979. Since then a multiplicity of divorce 'conciliation services' has been spawned, despite minimal government encouragement[2] and precarious funding. Even more recently there has emerged a plethora of mediation schemes in other spheres of conflict, including criminal justice and neighbourhood dispute.[3]

This development of 'informal justice' has been both dramatic and controversial. Alongside the various practice initiatives there has developed a body of criticism, anchored in the North American experience, which examines the political implications of this sudden growth in mediation and arbitration at the edge of the judicial system – see, for example, Abel (1982) and Auerbach (1983). It is claimed that these extra-legal forms have been foisted on the poor and weak – including black communities and women – in order, first, to frustrate collective responses to disadvantage, and second, to divert these vulnerable groups, who may be on the brink of achieving success through legal channels, into forms of second-class justice that lack the safeguards of due process. It is also argued that state control over people's lives, far from being diminished, is covertly extended through the proliferation of these informal mechanisms. These critics have examined the limitations of informal justice in such areas as landlord and tenant and small-claims courts and concluded that they are dominated by landlords and creditors respectively. It should be noted, however, that the application of 'informal justice' to the field of family disputes has not been expressly addressed in these accounts. To date, the only attempt to apply these lessons to the family sphere is that of Freeman (1984).

Meanwhile, the research that has been done on divorce mediation in Canada and the USA (Pearson and Thoennes, 1984; Irving and Benjamin, 1984) does not generally address the wider issues raised by this body of critical work in other fields. Of course, it could be argued that family mediation should not be criticized for failing to achieve what it never set out to do in the first place, that is, to help deal with underlying social and economic causes of oppression (Felstiner and Williams, 1985). But it is important, for example, to note the reservations that have recently been expressed by some feminist writers concerning the way in which conciliation in family disputes may collude with power imbalances related specifically to gender (Bottomley, 1984 and 1985). One must also acknowledge that court-based conciliation may involve covert regulation, operating in effect as a rationing device, denying access to judicial determination.

It is against this background that the work of the Bromley bureau must be assessed. We need to ask, for example, whether family disputes are a special category, for which mediation is particularly appropriate. Alternatively, do structural inequalities in the family sphere render these private agreements necessarily disadvantageous to women? And third, does the judicial system exert its coercive pressure on even 'out-of-court' mediation services?

Terminology

As already noted, the term 'conciliation' is a familiar one in the context of labour relations. It was probably first employed in relation to family disputes by the Finer Committee, reporting in 1974.[4] Although this committee was mainly concerned with court procedures, it also advocated extra-judicial processes which it termed 'conciliation'.[5] In making this recommendation it distinguished between 'reconciliation' and 'conciliation'. The former term was applied, as was traditionally understood, to 'reuniting persons who are estranged',[6] whereas 'conciliation', in what is by now its classic formulation, was defined as 'the process of engendering common sense, reasonableness and agreement in dealing with the consequences of estrangement',[7] and as

> assisting the parties to deal with the consequences of the established breakdown of their marriage, whether resulting in a divorce or a separation, by reaching agreements or giving consents or reducing the area of conflict upon custody, support, access to and education of the children, financial provision, the disposition of the matrimonial home, lawyers' fees, and every other matter arising from the breakdown which calls for a decision on future arrangements.[8]

'Conciliation', as thus described, represents a general approach to family breakdown, rather than a specific programme of institutional reform (Roberts, 1983). It incorporates two main features:

1 that family disputes should be resolved with the least possible bitterness or fighting;
2 that all the important decisions that have to be made following the breakdown of a marriage should be made, as far as possible, by the couple themselves.[9]

Whilst there are now a number of attempts to offer some form of 'conciliation' in disputes arising from marriage breakdown, the beguiling lack of precision with which this term is employed means that it is applied both to legal procedures and to a range of voluntary and statutory services, many of which vary greatly in organization, focus and in the spirit in which their activities are performed. It seems to us that the term 'mediation' more precisely encapsulates the essential features of a particular method of dispute resolution. It has a long history, particularly in North America, and, perhaps for that reason, greater precision in current use. It refers to a process whereby a third party, not identified with any of the competing interests involved and having no authority to *impose* a settlement, tries to help the disputants arrive at a negotiated outcome upon which they can both agree. The object, in other words, is to facilitate joint decision-making.

Whilst in Britain 'conciliation' and 'mediation' are often used interchangeably, we shall try to avoid any confusion by employing 'conciliation' only when referring to schemes' own accounts of what they do (or to the accounts of their umbrella organization, the National Family Conciliation Council) and when referring to the broad cluster of ideas first adumbrated by the Finer Committee. We shall use 'mediation' to refer more precisely to the specific form of third-party intervention that we have outlined.

Mediation distinguished from other forms of intervention

The characteristic that distinguishes mediation from other forms of dispute-resolution is that authority for decision-making remains with the parties. In this respect mediation differs from both arbitration and adjudication, each of which involves an appeal to an outside decision-maker. The parties engage in mediation voluntarily and the object is to arrive at an *agreed* outcome, this being the basis for the claim that these decisions are more likely to be adhered to than those that are imposed by a judge.

In *arbitration*, the parties to a dispute, by consent, invite one or more impartial persons to make a decision on an issue over which they themselves cannot agree. Arbitration awards are not legally binding, although the parties usually agree to honour the arbitrator's decision.

The *adjudicator's* authority is derived from the office which he holds (Roberts, 1979, p. 70). He imposes a decision by virtue of that office, rather than by invitation of the parties, and his decision is binding upon them. The adjudication typically follows a hearing attended by formal rules and procedure at which the parties face one another as adversaries and are usually represented by professional advocates. The outcome will often be such as to declare one a winner, the other a loser.

It is also necessary to distinguish between mediation and the kind of negotiation conducted by lawyers (whether solicitors or barristers) acting on behalf of their clients. In mediation, the negotiation is undertaken by the parties themselves, assisted by the mediator. However 'conciliatory' lawyers may be in the way they approach their dealings with other lawyers,[10] it is they who tend to control the pace and the substance of the negotiation.[11] The usual pattern, in fact, is for the legal advisers on each side to discuss the case together without the parties even being present. Many matrimonial disputes are formally 'settled' in this way.

Mediation must also be distinguished from those forms of intervention that are generally subsumed under the heading 'family therapy'. As one eminent practitioner has described it, 'Family therapy is not only a technical approach towards treatment . . . it is also a theoretical view of pathology giving rise to a whole range of treatment possibilities' (Walrond-Skinner, 1976, p. 6). The family therapist attempts to treat what is defined as a disorder (or 'pathology') within a family by changing the organization of that family and thereby altering the perceptions and behaviour of its members. In contrast, a fundamental assumption underlying the *mediator's* intervention is that the parties are competent, first, to define the issues for themselves; and second, to arrive at their own decisions following joint negotiation. The mediator does not regard marital breakdown and the disputes that flow from it as evidence of psychological dysfunction. Indeed, the parties are assumed *not* to be suffering from such a level of incapacity as might justify therapeutic intervention.

A second fundamental difference between mediation and family therapy is that the therapist assumes a leadership role, whereas the mediator does not. It has been said that 'the therapeutic contract must recognize the therapist's position as an expert in experimental social manipulation' (Minuchin, 1974, p. 111). But the mediator's expertise resides largely in his or her ability to ensure that the parties' right to manage their own affairs is recognized and protected.

It is true that some commentators distinguish between the use of family therapy techniques *in treatment* and their deployment in mediation (Robinson and Parkinson, 1985), but the reality of this distinction is questionable given that these techniques inevitably place the therapist/mediator in a very powerful position. It is also possible to distinguish between family therapy and a 'systems' approach to family conflict, but systems theory has largely been developed in the context of family therapy, so that this distinction is likely, in practice, to become blurred. One indication of this is the fact that, in 1983, the Institute of Family Therapy ran a course entitled 'Conciliation in Family Break-Up' in which it offered a 'family systems approach' whereby course members could develop 'family therapy skills in intervention'.

Having made these distinctions, we can turn to the question, in what circumstances should mediation be attempted? We would accept Fuller's suggestion (1971) that mediation requires 'an intermeshing of interests of an intensity sufficient to make the parties willing to collaborate in the mediation effort'. This 'felt sense of interdependence' creates a pressure towards accommodation and a recognition that differences are better viewed as open to compromise, rather than as requiring legal contest. Disputes arising from marital break-up involve intimate relationships – and what is more, relationships that are likely, through the presence of children, to continue into the future. Admittedly not all relationships, even continuing relationships, are based on shared interests (Silbey and Merry, 1986) so there may be occasions when the 'intermeshing' that is necessary if mediation is to succeed will not exist. But in the areas of marital separation and divorce it is likely that parents' concern for their children will motivate them to continue as far as possible in their parental roles. This in turn means that they will remain intertwined, with a common interest in co-operating over their differences (Kressel, 1985, chap. 1).

Conflicting objectives

By our account, the key aspiration underlying the development of extra-legal mediation services is that they should enable couples who would otherwise have to submit to outside decision-making to retain a greater measure of autonomy – and perhaps dignity – than is normally possible within the legal arena. This seems a worthwhile objective given that when a marriage ends, at least one partner is liable to have experienced the loss of a relationship they valued; they may also have lost, or be in the process of losing, their home and their children. Submission to the legal process, in which the parties have little opportunity to speak for themselves and are usually ill-equipped to 'give instructions' to legal advisers, may reinforce this loss of status and self-respect. Court adjudication is positively welcomed by some; but there is another group, the size of which can only be guessed at, who, whilst they cannot immediately agree matters between themselves, might be able, given sensitive and unobtrusive assistance, to retain a considerable measure of responsibility for the decisions that have to be reached.

Needless to say, the development of family mediation in this country reflects a much broader and more confusing range of objectives than is conveyed by the above statement of principle. Aside from any desire to promote party-control (and sometimes quite clearly at odds with it) one may discern four other arguments or ideas that have given life to the conciliation 'movement' in all its myriad, ill-defined forms.

First, it is thought that certain forms of conciliation may offer administrative and cost-saving advantages, for example in achieving a higher settlement rate of contested applications to the court (or reducing the number of such applications), thereby saving court time and perhaps achieving a corresponding reduction in legal costs. This preoccupation with 'savings' arises in part from the present climate of financial stringency; it reflects a view that the provision of legal services to a greatly increased number of divorcing couples, many of them with limited means, has become unreasonably expensive for the state.[12]

Second, conciliation has been identified with a greater concentration on the needs of children, bringing home to parents the hurt and perhaps even the long-term damage that may result from their continued quarrelling, or the abandonment of all links between the children and the non-custodial parent. For the past thirty years our divorce law has required that there be a judicial examination of the children's circumstances.[13] More recently it has been contended that divorce gives rise to a 'diminished capacity to parent' (Wallerstein and Kelly, 1980, p. 36). Many mediators are motivated, at least in part, by a perception that conflict between separated parents is bad for children; indeed, this is a quite explicit part of the case advanced on behalf of conciliation services (Parkinson, 1983). So it is possible to conclude that in the present enthusiasm for conciliation, we are witnessing an extension of the social-work practitioner's traditional 'child-saving' approach, albeit in a somewhat disguised form.

Third, conciliation has proved attractive to practitioners whose principal concern has been with the repair of family relationships, based on one of the many variants of the 'family therapy' model outlined above. Apparently, conciliation is regarded as an appropriate extension of these activities, if not actually synonymous with them (James and Wilson, 1986, p. 185). The tendency therefore is to regard it as a 'way in' to exploring the couple's relationships with one another and with their children. This goes well beyond the mediator's limited focus on *dispute* and involves the use of techniques that have not been explained to the parties, thereby failing to secure their informed consent.

Finally, there are those who emphasize the need for counselling and advisory services at the time of marital breakdown and regard conciliation as a means of meeting this need. Such a view is held by some members of the legal profession, perhaps because they continue to regard dispute resolution as their own preserve, whilst at the same time recognizing that people may need to talk through their problems with someone who has more time available than is usually the case with a busy solicitor. There is also a view that counselling is in any event best offered under the guise of dispute resolution because this has the advantage of being free from stigmatic associations (Murch, 1980, p. 35). Unfortunately, to regard counselling and advice-giving as forms of conciliation is likely both to blur the public image of mediation services and to distract the mediators from their primary task.

One can see therefore that as mediation is taken up by well-established agencies and interest groups, the idea that disputants may be helped to retain control over the outcome of their own quarrel is likely to be given less and less prominence; other objectives – therapeutic, administrative or child-saving – will tend to take over.

The failure to distinguish between these various approaches suits the purposes of professional bodies who are interested in staking a claim to this new territory. But the skills called for in mediation are not in fact the prerogative of any one professional group. Furthermore, if we accept that the most effective mediator is an unobtrusive figure, someone who operates *alongside* the parties (Roberts, 1983), this is at odds with our usual expectation of professional people, which is that they take over a problem and deal with it on our behalf.

Organization

There are at least four different organizational frameworks within which something called 'conciliation' is currently being practised. In terms of the various shifts of emphasis that we have outlined, these different frameworks will tend to promote their own particular modifications of the mediation idea.

The model that is probably least problematic is that of the completely independent conciliation service, such as that operating in Bristol (Davis, 1981). These independent schemes will tend to be used at an early stage in the dispute, often before a divorce petition has been filed. By and large, such services tend to have very low caseloads (BCFCS in Bristol is an exception) although this may change as they become better known. They tend also to have difficulty in attracting both parties to the dispute. Since they rely on local initiative, they enjoy varying levels of support from the legal profession and offer markedly differing services in many respects.

A second form of 'conciliation' is that which is undertaken by judge, registrar, or welfare officer, on court premises, as an integral part of the legal process. Several courts have developed such procedures on an experimental basis. These schemes are prone, needless to say, to the kind of 'administrative' distortion of mediation to which we have already referred. Indeed, it has been argued that the principle of party-control is inevitably diluted, if not lost altogether, in the course of this 'in-court' mediation (Roberts, 1983). It is certainly the case that these procedures have been introduced as a way of limiting the pressure on busy courts, rather than as a means of promoting parental autonomy. Interviews carried out amongst couples who have experienced these appointments suggest that little attention may be paid to the parties' own understandings and interpretation of their circumstances (Davis and Bader, 1985).

Third, many divorce court welfare officers refer to their undertaking a form of 'conciliation' in the course of a welfare enquiry ordered by the court (Shepherd, Howard and Tonkinson, 1984). Attempting to bring about agreement in the course of such an investigation is not new and this explains the view held in some quarters that 'conciliation' is something that these officers have always done. Certainly it is fair to say that welfare reports can act as a vehicle for achieving settlement; indeed, the conciliatory and even-handed approach of the welfare officer may, in some instances, enable a genuine accommodation to be reached. But it has to be acknowledged that welfare investigation and mediation have different objectives and are based upon different principles.[14] Even where the welfare officer sees his task, first and foremost, as helping to resolve a dispute between parents, the principle of party-control is bound to be undermined if the 'conciliator' may ultimately have to prepare a highly influential report for the court. Put simply, there is a risk that the welfare officer will use his authority in order to bring pressure on reluctant parents; the same problem therefore arises as in mediation on court premises.

Finally, there is the Bromley model, in which mediation is a discrete activity, clearly separated from the preparation of welfare reports. Although the conciliation bureau occupies the same premises as the divorce court welfare service, has the same person in charge and employs some mediators who, wearing a different hat, prepare welfare reports for the court, there is a strict information barrier between the two branches of the unit and no officer can 'mediate' in a case in which he or she may subsequently be asked to conduct a welfare investigation. Viewed in the context of the probation service as a whole, the bureau is a specialism within a specialism.

The South-East London Conciliation Bureau

The bureau is an 'out-of-court' service and focuses primarily (although no longer exclusively) on the resolution of access disputes (that is, disputes over the extent of, or the arrangements for, contact between a non-custodial parent and his or her children). Its practice is modelled on the organizational and theoretical framework developed by the American practitioner, O. J. Coogler, and expounded in his book *Structured Mediation in Divorce Settlement* (1978). For Coogler, the autonomy of the parties and the adoption of a 'modest profile' (p. 25) by an impartial intervenor are the key features of the mediation process, the ultimate objective of which is to enable the parties to reach an equitable agreement of their own, rather than have a solution imposed by a court.

Basic ground rules include a stipulation that the mediator will not engage in separate negotiation with either party. Children are not involved directly in the negotiation. The mediator assists in framing the agenda and ensures that both parties participate actively in the discussion. His or her most important task is to increase the flow of accurate and 'non-belligerent' communication. In order to achieve this he or she must maintain firm control over the manner in which the negotiations are conducted, although 'the best control is that which is least noticeable' (p. 26). It is not part of the mediator's task to offer help with underlying emotional problems.

Coogler's emphasis on a clear structure for the negotiation is intended to establish:

1 an orderly process, and therefore *procedural* fairness;
2 a commitment to certain ethical standards, including respect for the other person's point of view and a willingness to make full and honest disclosure;
3 security in the emotional environment, so that rational exchange is possible at a time when communication may well be poor (p. 79).

Needless to say, the need for transatlantic adaptation has led to a number of modifications of the Coogler model, the most obvious being the more limited focus employed at Bromley. Coogler was concerned with *all issues* attending separation and divorce; the Bromley bureau, in common with all out-of-court mediation services in the UK, deals mainly with issues relating to children.

Administrative arrangements

Divorcing or separating couples are referred to the bureau from a variety of sources, including the Croydon and Bromley County Courts, solicitors and Citizens Advice Bureaux. Welfare officers who have been asked to prepare a court report may also suggest to parents that they attend the bureau. Finally, many people take the initiative themselves, having heard of the service through the press or from other parents who have used it.

The co-ordinator of the bureau is also a senior court welfare officer. He has responsibility for maintaining the boundary between mediation and report-writing. Some of the divorce court welfare officers based at Bromley also act as mediators, but the majority of the bureau staff are drawn from outside the probation service. Of these, many work (or have previous experience) in social work, counselling or legal capacities.

In studying parents' response to the Bromley bureau, we are therefore examining one of the 'purer' forms of conciliation, but despite the clear focus on dispute resolution and the complex structural arrangements designed to prevent 'contamination' by the court welfare responsibilities also exercised in the unit, it would be surprising were the welfare service's predominantly child welfare orientation not, in some degree, to inform even the Bromley approach to mediation. Furthermore, since welfare officers are used to exercising authority (and since they have great influence with both the civil and criminal courts) some, at least, will find it hard to adapt to a mediating role. On the other hand, there is within the unit a clear understanding of the different approaches involved; the element of staff specialization amongst welfare officers, with only some of them engaging in mediation, is in itself an acknowledgement of this. So it is at least possible that the potential conflict between these various approaches may be overcome.

Research

Our monitoring of the bureau's work has taken place in two stages. The first of these, undertaken from January to May 1982, involved a study of the bureau's case records. We examined a total of 118 cases in which the parties had attended a joint mediation appointment at the bureau in the period from its inception in July 1979 to the end of March 1982. We also had extensive discussions with bureau staff and sat in as 'observers' on several mediation appointments.

Second, between July 1983 and February 1984 we interviewed 51 parents who had experienced mediation at the bureau. All these cases had involved an appointment attended by both parties. In 12 cases we interviewed both husband and wife and in a further 27 cases we interviewed one or the other. Accordingly, we gained 'consumer' evidence relating to 39 *cases*. We interviewed 27 men and 24 women.[15]

Before presenting our findings, we should acknowledge that cases referred to an out-of-court mediation service, mainly in order to resolve access issues, are unlikely to comprise a wholly representative cross-section of such disputes. It is not unreasonable to suppose that, on the whole, parents who are prepared to attend a voluntary mediation service are more willing to negotiate than are those (a small minority) who take their dispute as far as a preliminary court hearing, or a welfare report or even an adjudication. In a parallel investigation carried out amongst parties to contested proceedings in two county courts, it was apparent that many parents had not been able to contemplate negotiating together (Davis, 1988).

On the other hand, even amongst the latter court-based sample, there were those who told us that they *would* have been prepared to try mediation if only they had known such a service existed, or if this had been presented by their solicitors as a viable option. So in many instances they were not all that different from the Bromley group. Furthermore, whilst couples who accepted referral to the Bromley bureau had at least been prepared to be in the same room together, this certainly did not mean, as we shall see, that the dispute was relatively minor, or that there was not a great deal of bitterness between them. It was not uncommon for one or even both parties to assert initially that there was no prospect of a reasonable discussion with their former spouse – and yet in the end to conduct a satisfactory negotiation.

But to return to our initial point, the parents whom we interviewed in Bromley were rather more likely than those studied in the course of the court-based investigation to have met together in order to discuss aspects of their divorce, or to wish that they had done so. This suggests, just as we might have expected, that taken as a whole the bureau's clientele were slightly less entrenched. We have to take this into account when assessing client satisfaction with the various services they experienced. For example, there are bound to be comparisons drawn .between consumer views of the Bromley bureau and parents' response to 'in-court conciliation'. It has to be recognized that as far as the parties themselves are concerned, one is not necessarily comparing like with like.

Notes

1 ACAS (undated) *The ACAS Role in Conciliation, Arbitration and Mediation*, HMSO, London.
2 This lack of government will, at least in relation to 'out-of-court' services, was manifested in the *Report of the Inter-departmental Committee on Conciliation* (1983), Lord Chancellor's Department, HMSO, London.
3 See Marshall, T. and Walpole, M. (1985) *Bringing People Together: Mediation and Reparation Projects in Great Britain*, Research and Planning Unit Paper 33, Home Office, London.
4 *Report of the Committee on One-Parent Families* (1974) (Finer Committee) (Cmnd 5629), HMSO, London.
5 Ibid., para. 4.313.
6 Ibid., para. 4.305.
7 Ibid., para. 4.305.
8 Ibid., para. 4.288.
9 These ideas were elaborated in the *Report of the Matrimonial Causes Procedure Committee* (1985) (Booth Committee), Lord Chancellor's Department, HMSO, London.
10 The Solicitors Family Law Association Code of Practice (October 1983) clearly advocates a 'conciliatory' approach to divorce disputes. Solicitors Family Law Association, London.
11 The Booth Committee observed that 'Conciliation by its very nature emphasizes that the parties are jointly responsible for

dealing with the consequences of marriage breakdown . . . it is not a matter just to be left to lawyers' (Part III, para. 3.11).

12 Legal Aid expenditure in matrimonial disputes totalled over £71.1 million in 1984–5, as compared with £32.1 million in 1980–1. See the *35th Legal Aid Annual Reports (1984–5)*, The Law Society's Report, app. 4H (ii), HMSO, London.

13 This requirement was first introduced in 1958. It is now enshrined in the Matrimonial Causes Act 1973, s.41, under which courts have a duty not to grant a decree absolute without first declaring that the petitioner's proposals for the children's future are 'satisfactory or are the best that can be devised in the circumstances'.

14 The Booth Committee recommended the separation of report-writing and conciliation, commenting that these two activities 'are so different as to be incompatible' (Part IV, para. 4.62).

15 For further information concerning our research method, see Appendix II.

2

Dramatis personae

While the 51 parents interviewed at Bromley all figure at some point in this book, some accounts seemed to us particularly illuminating, reflecting as they did the experiences of many other of our informants. While not wishing to deny that 'each unhappy family is unhappy in its own way' (L. Tolstoy, *Anna Karenina*), these accounts illustrate what seem to us to be important general themes relating to marriage breakdown and the disputes that follow. We refer to these couples by name (not of course their *real* name) so that the reader may follow their stories through what is otherwise a thematic presentation. We treat eight cases in this way, in seven of which we succeeded in interviewing both parents. We have allowed them, as far as possible, to tell the tale in their own way. In this chapter we give something of the background to each case, concentrating on the period prior to their visit to the bureau.

Mr and Mrs Dennis

Mrs Dennis thought that she and her husband enjoyed a reasonably happy family life. When he left her for another woman, she was deeply shocked. As she said, 'I could not understand what was so fantastic about something else that he could, you know, reject what he'd had.' Underlying Mrs Dennis's reaction was her moral outrage at her husband's failure to abide by his marriage vows. Powerful and contradictory impulses governed her attitude to the break-up of the family. She felt that in leaving her, her husband was also leaving his children. In her eyes he no longer had any standing within the family. At the same time, she was demanding that he resume his share of the responsibility for the children's upbringing and disciplining.

Mrs Dennis deliberately sought out mediation as a means of settling these differences: 'One needs a neutral guardian angel to step in – someone not legal, not family, who has no vested interest, but is very aware of both sides.'

At the same time, she felt that too civilized a break-up concealed unfairness and created the impression that the destruction of the family was normal and acceptable – an everyday occurrence. This set a bad example to the children. She also considered that the parent who retained care and control had by far the heavier burden: 'Whatever guilt or remorse a non-custodial parent suffers, the daily grind of parental responsibility is incomparable – it takes all the pleasure away.'

All in all, Mrs Dennis was fired with a profound sense of injustice. She reckoned that there was a yawning discrepancy between the economic expectations of a wife and mother when the marriage was working and when it was not. Now, as sole carer for the children, her responsibility should be acknowledged and rewarded through generous financial provision. Instead, she was expected to find full-time work (she was already working part-time) in order to relieve her husband of his financial obligations. She believed that the true index of his commitment to his children was the financial one: 'I still think that if you bring children into the world, whatever you do about your own situation, you have a duty not only to them, but to the person who is supporting them and has their day-to-day care – and this is what he tries to extricate himself from.'

Mr Dennis was upset that his wife refused to allow the boys to visit or stay with him in his new home in the presence of his new partner. His solicitor recommended mediation, whereas Mr Dennis had been quite prepared to go to court: 'At that stage I wasn't going to the solicitor saying "Let's try and sort it out". I was saying I'd rather have an arbitrary decision of the court with all its risks, than this sort of arrangement.'

Nevertheless, he agreed to attend the bureau, his expectation of the meeting being that he would negotiate rationally with his wife over access.

Mrs Dennis, on the other hand, was determined to provoke an emotional response from him:

> Now my husband is, as you know, a civil servant. He's a typical paragon of Whitehall virtue. He never says three words when only one will do. And he had sat there during this interview and all I wanted, I wanted to get up and I wanted to shake him. I wanted to get some response from him. I didn't mind if he threw a chair in the room. I just wanted to get some response because I'd never had a response from him in two years. It had always been his sort of calm, calculated 'Anne, you're being typically emotional' – you know, all this sort of thing. I just desperately wanted [him] to start and *react*, which he hadn't done.

Mr and Mrs Lloyd

When this couple were referred to the bureau by the judge at the children's appointment, their situation could hardly have been worse. Over the previous six years, Mrs Lloyd had come to find her husband's violence more and more intolerable. She feared for the effect of this on her daughter as well as herself. However, for nearly a year after both parents came to believe that their marriage was at an end, no action had been taken by either of them, so overwhelming seemed the financial, practical and emotional difficulties of parting.

The already high level of hostility was exacerbated by the approach of their respective solicitors. According to Mrs Lloyd:

> He [husband's solicitor] instructed my husband not to pay anything, not to do anything, to fight everything, whereas on one or two occasions he may have been, for Jane's [child's] sake, a little bit easier if his solicitor hadn't been telling him 'don't', because for six months I didn't have a penny.

At the root of the conflict lay differing perceptions as to what constituted the proper amount of maintenance, and second, Mrs Lloyd's conviction that, for a while at least, there should be *no* access so that their daughter could recover from the effects of the break-up. The absence of direct communication between the parents placed a heavy burden on their daughter who had to act as go-between and take responsibility for initiating and arranging contact with her father.

Mrs Lloyd says that all she ever wanted was a happy home with lots of children. Instead, she found herself living alone with a deeply distressed and disturbed child. Though Mr Lloyd had remarried, he too continued to feel the effects of this accumulated bitterness in his new life, constrained as he believed it to be by the financial burden of his former marriage and anxiety over his daughter.

Mr and Mrs Parks

Mr and Mrs Parks married very young and Mrs Parks had always regarded her marriage as a happy one. When her husband embarked on another relationship within weeks of the birth of their second child, she felt that he had jeopardized everything – their family life together, their children, their material comforts – all the things that had constituted their happiness. She could not understand how he could do such a thing. In retaliation for this 'betrayal' and subsequent decision to leave, she deprived him of all contact with his children. This she saw as 'fit punishment'.

Mrs Parks also regarded her husband's new partner as a threat to what security remained to her. The matrimonial home represented the bedrock of that security and Mrs Parks was determined to fight any moves to sell the house.

Both parents felt that their solicitors tended to undermine any agreements they made and in general failed to respond to their problems with sensitivity. Mrs Parks in particular felt that these were personal disputes and had to be handled as such, but the approach of their solicitors had failed to reflect this. For her and her former husband, the visit to the bureau proved a turning point.

Mr Rice and Ms Harvey

This couple began cohabiting as students and had a young daughter. When their stormy relationship ended, Ms Harvey was determined to be independent of Mr Rice financially and in every other way. She refused maintenance from him, even for the child. When they came into conflict over access, they deliberately sought out conciliatory solicitors, each travelling long distances for the kind of legal advice that they wanted. They both said that they had simply wished to be informed of their legal rights.

Mr Rice's solicitor had dissuaded him from pursuing his claim for care and control:

> My legal advice was that it is very, very difficult for men to get custody, but that under the circumstances, if I wanted to, and bearing in mind that it would put the lid on *any* co-operation between us at all, and that lack of co-operation is the most damaging thing you could do, that they were certainly prepared to try.

Having given the matter considerable thought, he and Ms Harvey then turned to the bureau as a means of settling their dispute. Both were educated and articulate. As well as seeking to resolve their own difficulties, they were each interested in mediation as a process.

Mr and Mrs Robb

The effect of the break-up of this twenty-year marriage was devastating, especially for Mrs Robb. The only child, a young teenage daughter, was so distressed by the father's departure and setting up home with another woman that her school life was seriously disrupted and she needed professional help to enable her to cope. She refused to see her father in his new home and this was the main reason for his concern. He had on one or two occasions met his daughter by chance, whereupon she had turned and fled.

Mrs Robb felt that if she compelled her daughter to see the father, her own relationship with her would be jeopardized. However, she was not in principle opposed to access. She believed that the difficulties arose for two reasons: first, the complications of her husband's shift system, which made it difficult to arrive at any settled arrangement; and second, their daughter's own wish not to see her father during the course of divorce proceedings.

Mr and Mrs Selvey

Mrs Selvey was a widow of mature years with teenage children when she met and married Mr Selvey, a middle-aged bachelor. The marriage was unhappy from the start and they parted within two years, shortly after a daughter was born. Mrs Selvey believed that she was forced to choose between her children and her new husband, the clash between them being irreconcilable: 'I felt very guilty because I'd had a child and I don't really believe in divorce, you know. I was still sort of wavering, although I knew I had to have a divorce for the sake of my first children.'

Mr Selvey felt that as far as his wife was concerned, the accumulated stress brought about by a recent bereavement, overwork, moving house, adjusting to her new marriage, the reorganization of her family and the birth of a baby had, together, proved too much for her. He thought that she mistakenly blamed and sought escape from the marriage as a scapegoat for their troubles. Nevertheless, by Mrs Selvey's own account, the extrication from the relationship brought her nothing but benefit, whereas the opposite was the case for her husband.

The dispute over the child related to staying access. Mr Selvey explained his wife's objections to this idea in terms of her disappointment and resentment at the break-up of the marriage – this did not square with her being reasonable and co-operative in other areas. He believed that his daughter '. . . was being used as deprivation, as punishment – wittingly, or otherwise'. He carefully sought out a solicitor sympathetic to fathers' rights. However, this rebounded on him in that he subsequently felt that he was precipitately and unwillingly catapulted into acrimonious divorce proceedings with aggressively worded affidavits and a divorce petition that 'read like something out of the Nuremberg trials'. The judge at the hearing not only refused to grant him staying access, but cut his existing access by half.

Mrs Selvey claimed that if her ex-husband found a new partner, she would allow him more access as this would demonstrate that he was capable of normal relationships. Meanwhile the financial consequences of her failed marriage continue to cause her many regrets – loss of her widow's pension, children's allowance, and her late husband's retirement pension. She was particularly unhappy about the amount of maintenance awarded by the court:

> I was told that because it was assumed I would marry again, because I was reasonably attractive, that's why I wasn't given much maintenance, or so my solicitor said – which I found absolutely insulting. I feel very indignant about it and I find I'm getting more indignant as time goes on.

Mr Selvey for his part had sought what he called 'reasonableness' in dealing with the consequences of the marriage breakdown. He wanted equal rights, joint custody and frequent contact with his daughter. He received none of these things. As far as legal advisers were concerned, his account was one of ineptitude, negligence and injustice that has left him with an evangelical commitment to improve the lot of non-custodial fathers. Apropos of the performance of his solicitor, he remarked: 'If I'd have performed in the way he did, within my profession, I would be subject to an enquiry by the inspector.'

Mr and Mrs Bennett

This couple married very young. Mrs Bennett already had two children from a previous relationship and when she and her husband parted they had a baby son of their own. He became the subject of a bitter custody and access dispute. Both parents had new partners (a lesbian relationship for the mother) who jealously provoked them into far more combative attitudes than they would have adopted otherwise.

Mr Bennett had not wanted a divorce but was under the impression that the custody issue could not be sorted out independently. The legal process that followed seemed to him incomprehensible, generating a power of its own over which he had no control. He hoped that the meeting at the bureau would give an opportunity for him and his wife to discuss their differences face to face, and perhaps even to effect a reconciliation.

Mrs Bennett regarded her husband's tendency to violent fighting and rowing as the main problem. No one had been able to help her deal with this.

Mr Todd

We interviewed only the husband in this case.

Although both Mr and Mrs Todd had married new partners, they were still locked in dispute when they approached the bureau. The two children were living with their mother and Mr Todd felt that his access was being increasingly restricted. He was afraid that he was being deliberately and systematically excluded from the children's lives. One example of this was his former wife's wish to change the children's surname to that of their stepfather. The stress Mr Todd was experiencing was exacting a heavy toll on his health, personal relationships and work.

When this couple arrived at the bureau, their apprehension and insecurity had reached such a pitch that on first meeting there was an explosion of verbal antagonism.

Summary of general themes

At the time of their approach to the bureau most of these couples had experienced a severe deterioration in their personal relationship, to the point where the atmosphere in which they met was variously described as angry, bitter or strained. In no case could they be said to have been 'friendly'. For the majority, direct communication had virtually ceased, or else was attended by tension and 'rows'. The most extreme cases were the Lloyds and the Bennetts, for whom years of violence (witnessed by the child in the former case) had preceded their separation.

In some instances the manner of ending the marital relationship had contributed to this tension and mistrust. For example, in the case of Mrs Dennis and Mrs Parks, the husband's departure had come as a terrible shock. Both had believed their marriage to be happy and the sense of personal betrayal intensified the conflict over post-separation arrangements.

The experience of these two women was illustrative of another general theme in that older women with teenage children were less likely than their former spouse to have established a new relationship. This in itself engendered feelings of resentment and injustice and was in marked contrast to the sense of relief with which others in our sample (both men and women) had greeted the ending of their marriage.

Norms of 'fairness' or 'reasonableness' in relation to access (the length and frequency of visits, 'staying' access, etc.) varied considerably. Some custodial parents said that they opposed access on moral grounds: Mrs Dennis, for example, believed it wrong that her children should see their father living with another woman. Mrs Selvey, on the other hand, would have been more inclined to grant staying access if her former husband had demonstrated the emotional maturity required to sustain a new relationship.

The great majority of the parents whom we interviewed, both men and women, were very concerned about the effects of separation on their children. There was little evidence of the almost total self-preoccupation and lack of understanding of children's needs referred to in other studies (Wallerstein and Kelly, 1980; Mitchell, 1985). On the contrary, most parents were aware of their children's distress and were concerned to ameliorate it. One indication of this was that in two of the above eight cases parents had sought professional help for their child.

At the same time, these couples were not *only* concerned with the emotional suffering (their children's and their own) arising from separation and divorce; they also regarded adequate financial and material provision as being very important. The non-custodial parent's expression of concern for the children were regarded with scepticism unless matched by a willingness to share the responsibilities as well as the pleasures of child care.

3

The environment of mediation

The Bromley Conciliation Bureau describes itself as an independent agency.[1] But in seeking to offer a dispute-resolution service to separating and divorcing couples it has had to establish itself in a market place already crowded with legal and social work professionals. Furthermore, it has been dependent upon these other practitioners (solicitors and divorce court welfare officers in the main) for its supply of cases. In this chapter we examine this external environment, taking each group of practitioners in turn and drawing heavily on the experiences of the 51 parents whom we interviewed at Bromley.

Solicitors

All but two of our informants had consulted a solicitor about some aspect of their separation or divorce. This is consistent with the picture emerging from other research studies; solicitor consultation remains the norm, particularly if children are involved (Davis, Macleod and Murch, 1982). The fact that so many of the Bromley bureau clients had consulted a solicitor would also appear to confirm that mediation is regarded as an adjunct, rather than an alternative, to separate legal advice. This is hardly surprising given that the usual pattern is for mediation referrals to come *via solicitors*.

As resort to partisan legal advice continues to be regarded by the parties as the appropriate initial response to marital break-down, this puts solicitors in a very powerful position when it comes to determining which disputes may be passed to a media-tion service. Those solicitors who do refer cases (and it is only a minority who make referrals on a regular basis) focus primarily on the issues of access, care and control, and, to a lesser extent, on possible reconciliation in those cases where one party claims that the marriage is still viable. In regarding such disputes as particularly appropriate for mediation, solicitors almost cer-tainly have mixed motives. On the one hand, these issues are time-consuming, 'messy' and not very lucrative. But solicitors are also conscious of their own shortcomings when it comes to disputes with a high 'emotional' content; they may be convinced of the benefits of mediation for this type of problem.

It must also be understood that in referring this type of case, solicitors are falling in with the preferences (and presumed sphere of competence) of the mediators themselves. Access, custody and possible reconciliation are the issues that mediators – drawn, as they mainly are, from the ranks of marriage guidance counsellors, social workers and other 'wel-fare' professionals – feel competent to tackle. The publicity material prepared by mediation services, including the Bromley bureau, focuses on just these areas.[2]

The consequence of this partitioning is that within a given case, two sets of practitioners will be operating in parallel, although not necessarily in concert. Solicitors will be pursuing negotiation – and possibly litigation – on finance and property, even as they refer the access question to the bureau. So we find that in most Bromley cases the mediation process is encompassed by a legal framework that casts a very powerful 'shadow' over the negotiations, first, in the sense that all bargaining is influenced and circumscribed by decisions of the court and prevailing legal norms (Mnookin and Kornhauser, 1979), and second, through parallel legal proceedings and solici-tor negotiations – some of which may have a direct bearing on whatever matters are discussed at the bureau.

In interviewing former mediation clients, we gained considerable insight into the work of legal partisans. It was apparent, for example, that solicitors are often confronted by clients who are distressed, insecure and uncertain as to their objectives. But the solicitor can only operate within a legal framework. It is therefore tempting to push ahead with the divorce and so deny the client time to reflect on the course he or she wishes to pursue. This, for example, was Mr Selvey's experience:

> Two days after the initial break-up I just popped along for half an hour's assessment of my circumstances to a local solicitor. He started talking in terms of a kind of pro forma arrangement straightaway. He said 'Well, you know, obviously you're forty' or whatever it was, 'you need to rebuild your life again. You want a lot of free time,' he said. 'You don't want to be tied down . . . probably something like fortnightly, weekend access and perhaps certain holidays in the year.' He was lining me up for all this. Of course, I realize now this is what happens. It's all predestined and so on. I said 'No – I don't want to talk about that. I want to talk about ways and means of negotiating and sorting out some kind of reconciliation. . . . I haven't come along here just to sort of write it all off and set up. . . . I don't think that's appropriate at all, you know. I want a much more active relationship with my daughter, even if it is ultimately the case that the marriage is ended. But I don't want to begin by assuming that.'

Mr Selvey was not the only parent who felt that he had lost control over the conduct of his own case. This was the account of one custodial mother interviewed at Bromley:

> The problem was once I got to a solicitor, that was it, you're here for a divorce and nothing else. I at that time hadn't made my mind up and I said to them that I'd like a legal separation, but somehow I got the feeling that the solicitor would have preferred me to go and have a divorce . . . you know, get on with the nitty-gritty, complete, have a divorce. . . . On the other hand, I think it has happened for the better, really. I think it had to come to an end, but I was rushed by her, I'm sure. Because I went to her not knowing what to do. As I say, I didn't want a divorce.

Accounts such as these may come as a surprise to anyone who believes that, as a rule, solicitors move too slowly. But the point several of our informants wished to emphasize was not about speed as such; it was rather that they had been caught up in an excluding, alienating procedure that allowed them little opportunity to express their point of view. In some instances *both* parties experienced a feeling of impotence that amounted, in the most extreme cases, to a sense that they were almost irrelevant to what was happening around them. This was Mr Bennett's experience:

> The divorce, it wasn't what we wanted. I mean, like, we didn't agree on getting a divorce. . . . I fought for custody of my son and . . . it's something in the law which says before you can have custody you have got to be divorced. So, like, the day my wife received custody of my son was the day we got divorced. . . . It was nothing to do with us . . . divorce proceedings were going through. I mean, like, it was just a formality. Something that happened when you go to a solicitor.

It was a reflection of some parents' sense of being excluded from the decision-making process that they argued that solicitors should arrange 'foursomes', clients and solicitors sitting round a table together in order to try to reach an agreement. But despite many solicitors' endorsement of 'conciliation', this form of bilateral negotiation remains relatively uncommon. This reflects a view, common amongst solicitors, that what they have to offer is specialist legal knowledge – a technical competence that could be undermined through the bungling intervention of the parties; what they feel they *lack*, on the other hand, is the inter-personal skill that is needed in order to prevent a highly charged discussion degenerating into an acrimonious shambles.

Another suggestion was that parents should be able jointly to approach a solicitor. That such an option ought to be available is a view now gaining ground in legal circles.[3] This proposal is particularly interesting coming from clients of the Bromley bureau since it suggests that some couples would opt for joint legal advice *even though there are issues about which they disagree*. However, most solicitors are only too well aware of the risks involved in any departure from a strictly partisan stance. The woman quoted below had come to regard her wish for a joint consultation, in itself not unreasonable, as somehow bizarre:

> We're a very strange couple, Ted [husband] and I, really. Because he came to the first solicitor in Manchester *with me*, and what we wanted to do – it might sound weird, we wanted to see a solicitor together. And we wanted him to explain all the pros and cons of the situation. But a solicitor will *not* see you together. He's got this thing, he must act in the best interests of his client, so it was very, very difficult.

A clear message to emerge from our Bromley interviews was that these parents regarded quarrels arising from divorce as quite unlike other forms of dispute – that is, as 'human' problems of a very intimate kind, unique in each case. Something of this may be gathered from the reaction of this non-custodial father to the news that his solicitor was leaving, so his case would have to be passed to someone else in the firm:

> The second solicitor I went to see – she was okay, then one day I went to see her and she said 'I'm sorry, I won't be able to help you any more, I'm leaving to get married'. I thought, Jesus Christ, after all this time and all this sort of belief, then it's just cast aside. It just made me realize, that just like everyone else in the professions, it's just a job; it's no more than a job. And there you are, wasting your time, telling someone else your life.

The disappointment in this case could not have been avoided, but there were other instances where the solicitor's own manner suggested a failure to appreciate the importance of this relationship. Mrs Parks felt that the respective solicitors saw her and her husband 'as numbers, not as people that have feelings, or children, or anything . . . we're just another number on their book'.

That some solicitors should have these failings is unremarkable in itself, the most important point being that the parties obviously *look* to legal partisans for this emotional support; technical competence is not enough in itself. As Mrs Robb explained:

I didn't want to go cold to a solicitor who knew nothing about me. I mean, I couldn't have done that. I couldn't have said everything that I had to say in two or three visits. I needed a relationship with a solicitor. I needed someone to understand that I needed help.

Mrs Robb was fortunate enough to have found the help she was seeking: 'He's been a lot of support to me, a great support to me. He's allowed me to ring him any time at the office. And I feel that I can do that and I have done that.'

The divorce court welfare service

When there is a contested application concerning custody and access, or where there is some doubt as to whether the arrangements proposed for the children are satisfactory,[4] the court may order a welfare report. We found, in both Bristol and Bromley, that where there was dispute, most parents had initially been pleased that a report was to be ordered. As one custodial father commented: 'Now when this welfare officer turned up we were actually looking forward to somebody at last coming along and standing up for the children . . . because this is what Jill [step-mother] and I were trying to do.'

However, the way in which the welfare officers carried out this enquiry met with considerable criticism (Davis, 1988). The main problem had to do with the unsympathetic and judgemental attitudes that were often manifested. This was the reaction of one non-custodial parent, interviewed at Bromley: 'He was an arrogant pig. When I broke down and started crying, instead of being a bit sympathetic, he shouted at me, "Mrs H, can you speak!" in a very rough tone of voice.'

A father in another Bromley case remarked: 'He thought it was disgusting – oh yeah, we were all disgusting and all this sort of thing. . . . It became obvious to us that he didn't like us. It became obvious to us that he found us offensive and he didn't like our attitudes.'

Many parents felt prejudged and categorized:

Now from the word go he had already decided what this was all about. He hadn't met anybody. . . . Basically he came out with a lot of textbook stuff which didn't really apply to us as a family. . . . He was at a case last week where the grandfather was punched on the nose . . . and I said 'Well, that's nothing to do with us'. . . . He came out with a lot of stuff that didn't apply to us.

Welfare officers are meant to inform the court about the particular circumstances of each case, including any aspect of the relationship between parents and children that might influence the judge's decision with regard to access or care and control. Needless to say, this is a task calling for great sensitivity; it requires an ability to *discriminate* (in the sense of highlighting differences and idiosyncracies), but to many of the parents who experienced this investigation it appeared that the welfare officer had sought to stereotype and label. This was how one custodial father expressed his frustration:

They were defining access again, but nobody was taking into consideration the fact that there'd been this break, there'd been half a dozen visits in two years, there'd been aggravation, there'd been violence, there'd been threats. The children were in a terrible state and now they're saying, yes, you have got to send the children away with this person [mother].

Custodial parents complained frequently about the welfare officer's assumption that there *ought* to be some sort of access arrangement. In some of these cases the welfare officer's arguments were seen by parents to rest on deliberate mystification through the use of jargon or a spurious typology of post-divorce family problems. In other instances there did not seem to have been any particular arguments advanced:

When Emma [child] was asked whether she'd like to go out with dad, she said 'Well no, not really.' So [welfare officer] said, and bear in mind they're policeman's children, and all the time they've been brought up with 'What are you doing today daddy?' 'Oo, I'm taking a naughty man to see the judge'. . . . I mean, this is how you speak to children . . . this was how they were brought up . . . all of a sudden, [welfare officer] says 'Well, the judge' – who my children believe is something almost second to God – 'he might tell you that you don't know what is best for you, and he might tell you that you *ought* to see your father. Now what will you say to that?' My daughter's reply was ... she didn't really know what she was saying exactly, but she knew the gist of it – 'Well, I wouldn't mind once a month, or say every three months, or how about once a year.' Now that was put down on paper as Emma said she'd like to see her father. Well, that is tantamount to a bloody great big lie.

Following this report, the court made an order for access that, according to the mother, resulted in the children 'being forced all the time into situations which literally made them shake'.

In this, as in a number of other cases, it appeared that the welfare officer was simply anticipating what he took to be the *court's* view as to the desirability of access,[5] thereby, one might have thought, defeating the object of the welfare enquiry. There was also the suggestion that, just as the welfare officer volunteers the kind of information and views he believes the court will find acceptable, so the judge tends to support and protect 'his' welfare officer. This is a fact of life to which legal advisers become attuned, but that parents find difficult to accept or understand. As another Bromley parent remarked:

The poor old welfare officer ... with all due respect, he didn't get one fact on the report right. And I wanted to stand up in court and annihilate it. And I could have annihilated it, but the barrister's advice to me was 'I wouldn't do that, Mrs B, because the judge might not like having his welfare officer torn to pieces in court'.

The management of divorce disputes by professional third parties reflects a very uncomfortable blend of 'welfare' expertise and judicial decision-making. The divorce court welfare service represents an extension of the court's authority. Welfare officers also lay claim to a specialist body of knowledge and skills the parties do not have, in an area of conflict they regard as uniquely personal. Judging by these accounts, welfare officers do not seem particularly adept at conveying to parents that they are themselves 'experts' in their own case and should therefore retain a measure of responsibility for decisions that have to be reached. One of the objectives of our research into the Bromley bureau was to discover whether *mediation*, via a service that is closely linked to divorce court welfare and employs some of the same personnel, is any better at achieving this.

Notes

1 This description appears in the brochure prepared by the bureau:

> The Family Conciliation Bureau is an independent agency which provides a confidential and neutral forum where couples may discuss their disputes and reach their own agreements about custody and access with the help of skilled mediators. The aim is for arrangements to be made which are fair and satisfactory to the parties and their children.

2 In relation to Bromley, see Note 1 above. The Bristol service says of itself: 'BCFCS helps separating or divorcing couples to settle disputes, especially over children, and to co-operate with each other as parents'.

3 Lord Chancellor's Department (1985) *Report of the Matrimonial Causes Procedure Committee* (Booth Committee) HMSO, London, 1985. paras. 4.6 to 4.11.

4 Matrimonial Causes Act 1973, s.41. See Chapter 1, note 4.

5 This view was expressed in *M* v. *M* [1973] 2 All ER 85, when Wrangham J. stated that access was 'a basic right in the child'.

4

Inside the Bureau

'Conciliation', as far as the Bromley bureau is concerned, is understood always to involve a *joint* meeting between the mediators and the two parents. Children are not normally present (for discussion of this issue, see Chapter 10). The stress placed on this joint appointment, at least as a first step, may be compared with the approach of BCFCS in Bristol. A study of that service's case records revealed that amongst cases in which both parents were seen, only 27 per cent had involved a joint appointment (Davis, 1981).[1] At Bromley, parents are not given the option of meeting the mediators on their own. Direct comparison with the BCFCS workload would be misleading, given this fundamental difference of approach.

In surveying the history of the bureau, it is important to distinguish between the two periods: July 1979 to December 1980; and January 1981 onwards. In January 1981 the whole Civil Work Unit moved from Beckenham to Bromley and 'conciliation' was given a new lease of life. Of the 118 cases dealt with by the bureau over 33 months, only 33 (28 per cent) were referred in the 18 months prior to the move to Bromley. In 1981, 59 cases were referred and 26 in the first three months of 1982, suggesting a continued acceleration in the referral rate, at least up to that point. So after a slow start the bureau had, by the beginning of 1982, achieved a mediation workload (in terms of parents actually seen together) of about a hundred cases per annum.

This gradual increase in 'demand' is worth setting alongside the comments of the Inter-departmental Committee on Conciliation who observed that 'there is no evidence either that the demand for such services is large or that it will develop substantially'.[2] At the same time it must be acknowledged that low take-up, both in declining to accept an initial appointment and in failure to turn up on the day, remains a problem for most out-of-court, pre-litigation conciliation services, whether they be divorce court welfare run or independent. In part this reflects the fact that one or other parent may approach a mediation agency for *many* reasons, not necessarily in order to secure a genuine agreement with their spouse. Letters to the bureau declining the offer of an appointment often revealed a degree of scepticism regarding the other parent's motives in initiating the referral.

It has been calculated within the bureau that in 1981 one or other party failed to turn up for the mediation appointment in 33 per cent of cases. Of course, the *overall* 'refusal rate' is much higher, if one includes those parents who inform the administrator that they do not wish to participate. In 1981, 216 referrals were made to the bureau, the great majority with a view to mediation, although in some cases one parent may simply have been seeking advice on his or her own account. A mediation appointment was eventually held in 59 of these (27 per cent). Whilst this figure may appear disappointingly low, it is doubtful whether any other mediation service pursues such a rigorous joint appointment policy or achieves such a high proportion of joint appointments in relation to the number of cases initially referred. More recent perusal of the bureau's case records suggests that, in 1986, of 302 initial referrals, 146 (48 per cent) gave rise to a joint appointment.

Who refers?

The increase in the number of cases 'conciliated' between 1979 and 1982 probably reflects an improvement in take-up, arising from changes in the pattern of referral, as well as an increase in the number of initial approaches made. Of the parents interviewed in Bromley in 1982, 17 (33 per cent) told us that they had first heard about the bureau through their solicitor. The other major sources of information were the court and the divorce court welfare service. Sixteen parents (31 per cent) told us that they had heard of the bureau by one or other of these means. Other possible sources of information, accounting for comparatively few referrals, were the Marriage Guidance Council, Social Services departments, or Citizens Advice Bureaux.

In comparison with BCFCS, the bureau was at first rather slow to 'sell' itself to local solicitors. There were in fact only six solicitor referrals leading to mediation in the first eighteen months of the bureau's life. This perhaps reflects a professional blind spot concerning the key role of solicitors in guiding couples through divorce proceedings. BCFCS, with a management committee largely made up of lawyers, found it natural to turn immediately to solicitors in order to obtain work.

The number of cases referred by solicitors has gradually risen,[3] although the bureau still receives fewer solicitor referrals than does the Bristol service. It also attracts fewer self-referrals. On the other hand, the bureau has established close links with the Bromley and Croydon County Courts. This means that, compared with BCFCS, it tends to be referred cases that are at a slightly later stage in the divorce process.

Amongst self-referrals, the usual pattern is for the initial approach to be made by one or other parent, rather than by both together. In many cases, of course, the parents will not, at that stage, find it easy to communicate with one another. Indeed, if they could manage a joint approach they would perhaps be less in need of a mediator's help. But the fact that one parent has usually taken the initiative can give rise to considerable difficulties in terms of the other spouse's fear of manipulation, or of prior recruitment of the mediators. This is a problem many conciliation services fail to manage effectively and it may be one factor underlying their disappointingly low referral rate. BCFCS in Bristol do their best to get round it by encouraging *joint referral by solicitors*. (This can only work if both solicitors understand the basic principles underlying mediation.)

At Bromley, the problem does not arise in all cases because

some referrals come direct from the court or from a welfare officer. But in any event the service does not allow any individual discussion with a mediator prior to the joint appointment. Everything is done through the administrator. As far as the day-to-day running of the bureau is concerned, she is the lynchpin. She makes the appointments, assigns cases to the mediators and plays a key role in 'selling' the bureau to reluctant clients when they telephone or write in response to her initial letter. An appointment is usually offered within three weeks of the referral being made. This speed of response and the fact that there is virtually no backlog of work is in stark contrast to the practice of most divorce court welfare teams in relation to their report-writing responsibilities.

Pressure to attend

Attendance at the bureau is supposed to be voluntary, but this is less straightforward than might at first appear. As previously noted, the bureau shares premises and administrative staff with the divorce court welfare service. Eleven parents (21.5 per cent) told us that they were actually referred to the bureau by the court, or by the welfare officer assigned to their case. Six of the 11 told us that they had gone unwillingly to the bureau. One described her referral as being 'ordered' by the court. Others were not sure about this, but gained the distinct impression that they had had no option but to attend:

> I went . . . I think because we was kind of ordered to go by the judge. I'd rather not have gone. I'd rather have just talked to Ken [husband] on his own.

> The courts told us to go. And I said I wouldn't go and then I was told that if I didn't go, then I'd be put inside or something. I had a letter. . . . I was told I had to go.

> Well, I was told to by the court really. I mean, otherwise . . . they were having me as being disagreeable, which I suppose I was.

Several of these referrals were made by the judge in the course of the children's appointment held in accordance with the Matrimonial Causes Act 1973, s.41. One father explained that the judge had insisted that he went to the bureau because he was not satisfied with the proposed arrangements: 'The judge refused to give the decree until we'd been to the conciliation and sorted out the problems with the children. Once he was happy with that and received a report from the conciliation, I think then it was the absolute.'

A father in a different case had refused to keep an appointment made by his wife, only to find that the court 'ordered' him to attend: 'That's why I went to the FCB to tell you the truth. I was ordered to . . . it came from the judge through the clerk who wrote to my solicitor. She wrote to me and said, "you'll have to go this time".'

It is doubtful whether a judge can actually 'order' parents to attend an out-of-court mediation service, although a recent Practice Direction instructs judges and registrars 'to consider referring contested cases to local conciliation services where these exist' (*Family Law*, 1986, p. 286). It is tempting for mediation services to foster these ties with the court: first, because it may be thought status-enhancing (certainly true in relation to solicitors, and possibly in relation to the parties as well); and second, because the court may prove to be a significant source of new cases. The Bristol service employs the term 'Courts' in its title, apparently in the belief that a satisfactory caseload can only be achieved through a link with the prestige and authority of the court, even if that link is illusory. Likewise at Bromley, the perceived need to demonstrate high caseloads and a high 'success rate' in order to sustain Home Office and probation management support acts as a pressure in the direction of closer collaboration with the courts.

It is not surprising therefore that some Bromley parents referred to the bureau by the court do not distinguish between the report-writing function of the court welfare service and the role of the bureau. This is despite all the efforts to establish the separateness of mediation. One mother had regarded the mediation appointment as just another interview in a series of six or so which she had with staff of the divorce court welfare service. Another woman's dissatisfaction with the welfare officer coloured her attitude to the bureau, despite what she regarded as her sympathetic treatment there. The officer preparing the report had referred her to the bureau: she felt that he had put pressure on her to reach agreement through mediation by spelling out a totally unacceptable alternative which, it was claimed, would be imposed by the court if the dispute were not resolved.

It was unfortunate in each of the above cases that greater efforts were not made to separate off the bureau's activities. But one can well understand why some parents might be reluctant to accept that there is a genuine communication barrier between two services. After all, some members of staff undertake both tasks (albeit not in the one case) and the two services are based in the one building. Parents' scepticism may also be well founded in so far as it is a response to the practice of other welfare agencies. Even in relation to BCFCS, a service much more clearly independent than the Bromley bureau, one or two parents confessed to a vague unease, as if they did not really believe that a service operating on the margins of the legal and welfare structures could ever be truly confidential.

The uncertainty that is felt by some parents on this point is shared by some academics who have expressed reservations about the development of extra-legal mechanisms for resolving divorce disputes (Freeman, 1981). One of the tasks for this research was to discover whether party-control was undermined to such an extent that the activities of the bureau (and, one might infer, of other mediation services) actually involved an extension of social control and increased intervention in people's lives.

The setting

The conciliation bureau is situated in a large Victorian house in a quiet residential area of Bromley. Separate waiting rooms are available, as is a playroom. These pleasant surroundings and the reasonable standard of decor within the building are important in defining client status.

The general atmosphere of friendliness in the office was well received by parents, as was the practice of allowing them to wait in separate rooms. Indeed, the only criticism of these preliminary arrangements came from one mother who, contrary to the general practice, found herself in the same waiting room as her husband. He had been violent towards her in the past and she had sought reassurance from the bureau that she would be protected. It was very unnerving therefore to find her husband sitting beside her as they waited. Apparently, the tension was acute. In this woman's eyes, the situation was saved only by the protective presence of her second husband, which meant that serious confrontation was avoided.

The meeting

Wherever possible the mediators work in pairs, one male and one female. The actual negotiation takes place in three phases. First, there is a brief meeting of parents and mediators together at which introductions are effected and the framework and purpose of the exercise are outlined. Then the parents are seen separately in order that they may each give their side of the story without interruption and, in effect, say what *they* want to get out of the meeting. The third stage – that of joint negotiation – begins with one or other of the mediators briefly summarizing the points made by the parents when spoken to on their own.

The way in which the mediators embarked on the appointment met with general approval. Parents were often feeling tense and they appreciated the efforts made to put them at their ease: 'They showed us into a nice office, sat us down. . . . [Mediator] made you feel very welcome actually. He went out, got a tray with four cups of tea and brought it in, tea and biscuits, which sort of instantly made you relax a bit.'

This is the stage when the mediators emphasize the confidentiality of the discussion, tell the parties that no prior information about them has been received, and describe the independence of the bureau from other agencies. In addition, they ask the parties for permission to stop exchanges should they become destructive or too upsetting.

Phase two – the mediators seeing each parent separately – was also regarded as very important. The following account was typical: 'It [the whole appointment] made me very anxious actually. I was really relieved when they saw us separately. It was really necessary, that. That I think was the most valuable thing actually. Because that meant that both of us had our say.'

Viewed as a whole, the conduct of the appointments is now much more flexible than in the early days of the bureau, although still adhering to the basic structure adapted from Coogler's model. For example, the original injunction that the preliminary discussions with each parent last for 'seven minutes' has long since been abandoned, as has any strict time limit on the appointment as a whole. But the essential pattern – the three phases outlined above – has been retained. The aim is to provide a framework within which parents feel protected, so that each has an opportunity to state their case and, subsequently, to negotiate. It is impossible for fairness to be guaranteed by means of these structural arrangements, but it would seem right that the proceedings be made as *demonstrably* fair as possible.

There is also an important point to make about the mediators' report-back at the start of phase three. This is based entirely on what they have learnt from the parents. The object is to clarify issues *as these are perceived by the parties*. It is characteristic of the bureau's mode of operation that, apart from parents' names, no prior information about the family is vouchsafed to the mediators. This is in marked contrast to most social work (including divorce court welfare) practice, where it seems generally to be held that the more information that is available, the better. To this extent the confidential nature of mediation operates in both directions, restricting the information that comes in, as well as that which may be passed on. This restriction is very important in reminding mediators that they have a purely facilitating role.

Number of sessions

It was originally envisaged that the bureau would offer only one appointment per case, but this pattern has also been modified. It is now quite common for parents to be encouraged to return for a second or even a third meeting, either to check on progress, or to negotiate the next phase following some interim arrangement.

Amongst our interview sample, we discovered that in 23 of the 39 cases (59 per cent) there had been only one appointment at the bureau; that is to say, the parents had attended together, on one occasion, and neither had made a return visit. In the remaining 16 cases, one or both parents had attended a second time.

Having opted initially to allow only one negotiating session per case, there was some uncertainty within the bureau as to whether this should be modified. On the one hand, it was recognized that a second appointment might be needed in order to check on some trial arrangement. It was also felt that where there was a great deal of bitterness or hostility, the movement being asked of people might sometimes be more than could be encompassed within the one session; accordingly, there was a risk that an 'agreement' would be purely cosmetic, reflecting the time pressure the parties were under. There was also a feeling that too much stress might be placed on the mediators in the course of the one, highly concentrated negotiating session.

On the other hand, it was argued that a shift towards a more leisurely (as well as more familiar and perhaps more comfortable) work style would lead to a loss of urgency and focus in the initial appointment. The need for a further meeting could be said to imply a lack of 'discipline' (as one mediator described it) in the first session. There was a general reluctance to move in the direction of a more protracted, counselling-type relationship. It was also feared that some mediators, in their desire not to admit failure, would do all they could to avoid 'losing' a couple who were unable to reach agreement, hoping against hope that something would be achieved next time.

Although the bureau's focus on a single negotiating session is less clear cut than was originally the case, the continued emphasis on the one tripartite meeting still makes it unusual amongst mediation services. BCFCS, for example, has never had such a policy. Indeed, the Bristol mediators, as with many other services, tend not to even consider a joint appointment until they have had preliminary meetings with each parent separately.

For the most part, the parents whom we interviewed at Bromley appeared to accept and respond to the mediators' expectation that they try to negotiate an agreement at the first meeting. On the other hand, there were occasions, as we shall see, when the negotiations followed a rather unpredictable course over two or three sessions. In a few instances an apparent consensus was reached at the first meeting, only for this to be rudely disrupted on a second visit. Equally, it might have taken up to three appointments for a workable agreement to emerge.

Mr Rice's viewpoint was fairly typical, in that he regarded the possibility of a further appointment as a kind of safety net:

> In retrospect, I think it was OK. I had reservations at the time, but they said to me, well, look, you know, we're trying to work out an arrangement. Let's try this. Maybe it's worse than what's gone before, but we're trying to sort of work towards something better. And that is the situation where you feel if somebody's not being quite fair you can go back and say 'Well, look, I think what you said on such and such occasion wasn't fair'. So I mean – which *is* fair . . . we were encouraged to go back if necessary.

It was important to Mr Rice, as to all the bureau's clientele, that he be treated fairly. The flexibility which the mediators were prepared to build into their negotiating structure contributed to this. Nevertheless, it is clear that most of the hard work of negotiation had taken place at the first meeting:

> By the time we came back the second time, really the problems had been solved at that first meeting, simply by saying 'Well, OK, you know, this is the agreement.' And from then on it was much smoother. It sounds almost – maybe I'm sort of constructing something here – it sounds almost miraculous – but emotionally it became much less fraught. We'd solved the problem over access and a lot of other things at the same time.

Notes

1 It has to be said, however, that this research was undertaken in 1979–80, in the twelve months immediately following the scheme's transition from 'experimental' to fully-funded status. The proportion of joint appointments may well have increased since then. Indeed, of 48 former BCFCS cases we came across during the 1982–83 study based on Bristol County Court, 19 (39.5 per cent) had involved a joint meeting at some stage.
2 Inter-departmental Committee on Conciliation (1983) Lord Chancellor's Department, para 5.7, HMSO, London.
3 Of 363 referrals to the bureau in 1985, 101 (28 per cent) were made by solicitors.

5

Issues and outcomes

The publicity material disseminated by the Bromley bureau has focused almost exclusively on the access question. This concentration on access disputes has come about for several reasons: first, a belief that a failure to agree access arrangements is probably the most common type of dispute between parents following separation; second, a view that the failure to resolve this issue causes unhappiness and perhaps long-term damage to children; third, a belief that access quarrels may be more amenable than other divorce disputes to mediatory intervention; and finally, a perception on the part of the mediators that it is in this area that they can claim most expertise and therefore have most to offer parents.

Forty of the parents whom we interviewed at Bromley (78 per cent) told us that their visit to the bureau had been prompted solely by difficulties over access. The following is a typical statement (from the non-custodial parent's point of view) as to what was being sought from the bureau:

> I wanted to be able to see my daughter. I hadn't seen her for a long while. I knew there were problems. My wife and I

couldn't sort it out. There was no way that I wanted to insist on my daughter coming to see me. . . . I don't think my wife would have wanted that either. So I just hoped the conciliation bureau would bring us together again. I had no idea what the conciliation bureau was at all, you know, but anything that would help I would obviously try.

But in other cases the picture was more complex, the initial approach having been prompted by a range of difficulties or aspirations. Access difficulties featured in almost every bureau case, but in addition five people told us that they had wanted to explore the possibility of a reconciliation, while others mentioned money and property, or a dispute relating to care and control.

It was apparent that parents did not always share a common objective. For example, there were three cases in which the wife said that she only wanted to negotiate on access, whereas the husband laid particular stress on the possibility of a reconciliation, with access difficulties being very much secondary. As Mr Bennett explained:

At that time I think I expected miracles because I expected to walk out of there with some hope that we might be able to get back together again, or at least we might have been able to talk, but we went away from there the same way as we went in, with nothing gained.

It was difficult for us to judge how realistic were the hopes of reconciliation still being harboured in such cases. Accounts such as the above would suggest that by the time the bureau was approached, there was very little prospect of saving the marriage. However, this may be a superficial judgement. BCFCS has claimed a 'reconciliation rate' of 17 per cent (Parkinson, 1983) and amongst our Bromley interview sample of 39 cases, two couples were in fact reconciled some time *after* their visit to the bureau. Even Mr and Mrs Bennett are now on much better terms than at the time of their mediation appointment.

It has to be recognized that many people feel very ambivalent about trying to save their marriage. In the following example the husband claimed that he had wanted a reconciliation, but he obviously felt so bitter towards his wife that it appeared he was seeking an opportunity to recriminate as much as anything else:

I hoped to achieve going back together. I hoped to achieve that but I didn't really think it was going to happen because from the outset really, I didn't really trust my wife. If I thought, you know, there was some mental blockage which meant that we would never get together, I was hoping maybe the mental blockage would clear, but it hasn't done. She wasn't after any reconciliation with me. Her main concern was to see the children, because I think we'd already been to the courts and she hadn't got her way there so she was looking to the next one down the line to see if she could get her way there. . . . I wasn't worried [about access] – the children were with me.

This couple had been seeking different things from the bureau, so it is perhaps not surprising that the mediation attempt was not a success. Unfortunately, renewed contact through the bureau re-activated the husband's belief that reconciliation was, after all, a possibility. It also refuelled his anger and distress at being rejected yet again.

Whilst the possibility of reconciliation remains a live issue in some cases, it is clear that the mediators regard their main task as that of helping parents reach agreement over access. In comparison, the divorce court welfare service has a much broader brief, including the preparation of 'satisfaction' reports for the court in cases where there need be no dispute between the parents. Furthermore, in cases that *do* involve disagreement between parents, welfare officers have traditionally been more concerned with the issue of care and control. (Some of the welfare reports which we studied at Bromley barely alluded to the access question.)

So it is clear that the setting-up of the bureau reflects a shift of focus. The traditional issues – care and control and child welfare (or 'satisfaction' in the court's terms) – have a kind of unchanging and unchangeable quality about them. They are problematic no doubt, but not very easily modified from the outside (Eekelaar *et al.*, 1977). The purpose of welfare investigation in such cases may not be to change anything very much, since nothing much can be changed; it may be designed instead to demonstrate fulfilment of the state's responsibility to protect the interests of children on their parents' divorce. Disputes over access are more likely to be open to outside influence. The situation is often fluid. Some degree of co-operation between parents is required if access is to work at all. The authority of a court order is of little use in these circumstances.

Less tangible objectives: altering the balance of power

In addition to various practical objectives, mainly concerned with the access question, parents had a number of other, less concrete aspirations, for example, a desire to influence the attitude of the spouse in the course of access handovers, or a wish to recover control over the separation arrangements, this having been lost in the course of legal proceedings.

The latter point is the most interesting. Some parents clearly saw mediation as a kind of 'middle-way' between direct husband–wife negotiation (which had not worked in their case) and court adjudication. As it was put to us by one of the men interviewed in Bromley:

> We thought there should be something between two people talking and a court hearing. We thought there must be something inbetween, surely . . . we didn't want something as drastic as court, but the two of us, one to one, wasn't working. You actually go from one extreme to another. You go from one extreme where you actually . . . at that stage I couldn't talk to her about anything . . . and at the other end of the scale, at court, it's taken out of your hands anyway.

Underlying many bureau referrals is the view of one parent (or possibly both) that he or she is at a disadvantage in terms of current negotiating strength. These disadvantages may be of different kinds – for example, in being economically or emotionally vulnerable; in having a weaker case in law, or a weak solicitor; or, for the non-custodial parent, in having a less powerful voice in determining access arrangements. The following extract hints at one or two of these themes, which we develop in Part Two, as part of our examination of the mediation process:

> I hoped to receive a fair crack of the whip because up to that day I believe I'd never had one because my ex-wife was

fortunate enough to have a bloody brilliant solicitor, there's no doubt about it, he was brilliant; and I just had a Mr Average. Plus, she being a woman, with the child, you know.

Outcome of the appointments

There is clearly a limit to the weight one should attach to a measure of outcome based on a single mediation appointment. It was apparent from observing some appointments at Bromley that 'agreements' could be extremely tentative, with much work remaining to be done by the parents themselves. Even where a firm commitment was entered into, the residue of bitterness and mistrust between the parents may have been such that it would not take very much to upset it. It would clearly be unrealistic to expect one – or even several – mediation appointments to restore harmony in such cases. Nor can a simple measure of agreement fully take account of the different levels of conflict presented to the bureau. Where the couple are very entrenched, an agreement to continue talking may be as great a step forward as an agreement on the substantive issues in a less difficult case. With these reservations in mind, Table 5.1 shows the outcomes, *as recorded by the mediators*, in the 118 cases examined in the course of the 'files' study at Bromley.

Table 5.1 Outcome of mediation appointments

		(n = 118)
Agreement reached	45	(38%)
Some progress	29	(25%)
Uncertain outcome	15	(13%)
Failure to agree	27	(23%)
Not recorded	2	(2%)

The proportion of 'agreements' had altered over the life of the bureau. This becomes apparent if cases are divided into three groups, according to the date of initial referral, as in Table 5.2. On the basis of the mediators' record of outcome on the day, there seems to have been a significant improvement over the life of the bureau. The factors most likely to account for this are:

1 changes in bureau personnel;
2 changes in the type of case and source of referral (in particular, the growing number of solicitor referrals);
3 increasing skill on the part of mediators.

Table 5.2   Outcome within different time periods

	Referred in 1979–80 (n = 33)		Referred in 1981 (n = 61)		Referred from January 1982 (n = 24)	
Agreement	7	(21.0%)	24	(39.0%)	10	(42.0%)
Some progress	6	(18.0%)	17	(28.0%)	6	(25.0%)
Uncertain outcome	5	(15.0%)	5	(8.0%)	5	(21.0%)
Agreement followed by breakdown	—		4	(6.5%)	—	
Failure to agree	14	(42.5%)	10	(16.0%)	3	(12.5%)
Not recorded	1	(3.0%)	1	(2.0%)	—	

As far as our interviews were concerned, parents reported that an agreement was reached at the bureau in 22 out of 39 cases (56 per cent). This corresponds with 'agreement rates' reported in American studies of family mediation (Pearson and Thoennes, 1984). An interim agreement was reached in two cases (5 per cent) and no agreement was reached in the remaining 15 (38.5 per cent). We compared these results with the mediators' own record of the appointments contained in the bureau case files. The only significant difference was that the mediators recorded a number of equivocal outcomes that we had to categorize as 'uncertain' or 'some progress'. Parents tended not to do this. That aside, there was a good 'fit' between outcome as recorded by the mediators and that recalled by the parents themselves.

The fact that parents and mediators shared a common view about what had gone on distinguishes these appointments from attempts at 'mediation' on court premises (Davis and Bader, 1985). Another reassuring aspect of the Bromley findings was that in the twelve cases we interviewed both parents, there was an almost perfect 'fit' between the two accounts in terms of whether or not an agreement had been reached. Again, parents' accounts of the outcome of in-court conciliation appointments at Bristol County Court were much less congruent than this (Davis and Bader, 1985).

Outcome matched against source of referral

The highest level of agreement was recorded in cases where the parties had been referred to the bureau by their solicitors. (Of 13 such cases in our interview sample, there was an outright agreement in eight, with an interim agreement in a further three, a 'success rate' of 85 per cent.) Self-referrals, or cases referred by the court or the divorce court welfare officer had 'agreement rates' of between 50 per cent and 60 per cent.

The fact that cases referred to the bureau by solicitors had a higher overall level of agreement than did self-referrals is not surprising. In the course of an earlier study of BCFCS, it was noted that cases referred by solicitors were associated with both a higher level of take-up and a higher agreement rate than were self-referrals (Davis, 1981). In part this reflects solicitors' ability to select out appropriate cases; second, it may indicate that having initiated the referral, solicitors actively support the efforts of the mediators; third, solicitor referral may counteract any suspicion on the part of the 'non-referring' parent that he or she is being manipulated by 'the other side' (see also Pearson, Thoennes and Vanderkooi, 1982).

It is also important to note that despite the pressures that might be experienced by couples referred to the bureau by the court, or even by the divorce court welfare service, these cases were associated with a lower level of agreement than were those referred by solicitors (where one might suppose that there was less risk of coercion). This, together with the evidence presented in Chapter 4, suggests that the pressures placed on parents by the court sometimes proved counter-productive.

Developing this theme, we find that self-referrals, despite their modest agreement rate at the bureau, were more likely than either solicitor or court referrals to result in access continuing to take place up to the point of our interview. This may reflect a deeper reservoir of goodwill (or stronger motivation) amongst the self-referred group. At the time of the mediation appointment this may have been less potent than the pressure exerted by solicitors or the court. However, it may have

reasserted itself over succeeding months. This is the best explanation we can think of for the fact that while several of those
other agreements broke down, many 'self-referred' parents
worked out their own arrangements some time *after* their visit
to the bureau.

Outcome matched against stage of divorce proceedings

We found that there was a significant difference in 'success rate',
depending on whether or not the couple were already divorced at
the point when the mediation appointment took place. The
breakdown in Table 5.3 is based on our interview sample; we
exclude cases where the couple were subsequently reconciled,
or where the question of divorce did not arise because they were
unmarried.

The high agreement rate achieved with the already divorced
matches the picture we found when studying the outcome of
cases at BCFCS. We noted in the course of that study that
couples referred for mediation after they had been awarded their
decree absolute were much more likely to reach an agreement
(Davis, 1981). Certainly it is by no means clear that mediation in
the very earliest stages of the dispute (as is often advocated)
achieves the best results.

One obvious explanation for this pattern is that disputes that
arise some time after divorce will be less fraught than those that
occur in the immediate aftermath of the marriage breakdown. It
is also likely by that stage that only one issue will be involved,
so that the quarrel will tend to be more manageable. Certainly it
was characteristic of the post-divorce cases referred to BCFCS
that they involved only the access issue (Davis, 1981).

Table 5.3 Outcome matched against stage of divorce proceedings

	Divorce prior to attending bureau (n = 15)	Divorce obtained after attending bureau (n = 20)
Agreement reached	12 (80%)	7 (35%)
Interim agreement	—	2 (10%)
No agreement	3 (20%)	11 (55%)

Influence of new partnerships on the outcome of mediation

Our figures also suggest that where parents (one or both) had embarked on a new relationship, agreement was rather more likely to be reached at the bureau. Thus, of nine cases in which we were told that *both* parties had either remarried or had formed a new relationship, seven had resulted in agreement (78 per cent). This compares with an agreement rate of around 40 per cent where only *one* spouse was said to have formed a new relationship, and 20 per cent (admittedly in respect of very few cases) where *neither* party was said to have done so. (Forming new relationships is, to some extent, a function of time and so this finding should be set alongside the previous point concerning the higher agreement rate following divorce; it is not clear which of these two elements has the greater predictive power.)

Some parents mentioned the significance of new partners, not so much because of the part they played in their own lives, but rather because of their importance as step-parents to their children. The woman who had been relieved that her new husband was present in the waiting room, believing that this was necessary in order to protect her from her former spouse, felt that her new partner's presence also contributed to the success of the negotiation. The relationship with her former husband became much more relaxed following the mediation session. The new partner now acts as an 'agent' between the parents, facilitating arrangements and providing a calming influence.

On the other hand, a few parents complained that the mediators had attached too little importance to a new partner's role in relation to the children. In some of these cases the mediators had been faced with an awkward situation in that this new husband or wife had been brought along to the bureau, only for the other parent to refuse to allow him or her to play any part in the negotiation. In these circumstances, of course, this new relationship may well have contributed to the ill-feeling between the parents. On the other hand, the new partner's responsibilities in relation to the children are bound to figure in the discussion, so it might seem sensible to allow him (or her) to contribute directly. But for the unaccompanied parent, faced with this decision at the start of the appointment, the direct involvement of their former spouse's new partner may represent a major concession; it may appear tantamount to losing the argument before they start.

Conclusion

We have given some indication of the outcome of these cases in Part One since this provides a necessary backcloth against which to judge the parents' more detailed accounts of the mediation process. However, there is no one criterion by which success can be measured and these 'objective' yardsticks are meaningless without a fuller understanding of parents' experience at the bureau. It is asking a lot that a two-hour appointment should have a dramatic impact upon what may be a long-standing family quarrel, so what we must try to do is assess whether any kind of positive influence was exerted, and second, arrive at some understanding of the ingredients that contributed to mediation being regarded (by some parents) as a genuinely helpful experience.

PART 2

The process

6

Mediators and parents

Whilst the Bromley bureau lays down a broad framework within which the mediators perform their task, there remains considerable scope for individual variation reflecting the personal attributes of mediators and of parents. Differences of expectation, of worker style (Brown, 1977), of 'ways of seeing' a particular problem – all will play a part in determining the conduct and outcome of a given mediation session. These elements are explored briefly in this chapter because we feel it important to acknowledge the extent to which the personal qualities of the participants contribute to the success or otherwise of a negotiation.

Mediators

The bureau has used a considerable number of mediators (some twenty or so since it opened in 1979) so it would be surprising were we *not* to find that different mediators were seen by parents as possessing different levels of skill and aptitude for the task. For example, in response to our question asking whether the mediators had been 'good at their job', three parents distinguished between the two mediators in their case, claiming that one had been effective whilst the other had not. Similar differences were remarked upon by parents who had experienced more than one appointment, sometimes with different mediators at a second or third session. One woman told us that the first interview was conducted in such a way as to make her feel under cross-examination. She thought that the mediators were trying to catch her out; if you were feeling 'down', they would make you quite depressed. At the second interview there was a different woman mediator and she was much more understanding.

This is only one small illustration of the differences of approach that were perceived by parents and that no doubt influenced the outcome of the proceedings. At the same time, we would not claim to discern any very obvious pattern, with some mediators ranking 'high' and others 'low'. On the contrary, it appeared – at least in relation to the comparatively small number of mediators (six or so) who have undertaken the majority of work in the bureau – that different 'sets' of parents (and indeed, individual husbands and wives) quite often arrived at sharply contrasting judgements regarding a particular mediator's style and effectiveness. This should not surprise us too much. From a research point of view it suggests a possible limitation to processual accounts when these emanate from just one set of actors in the drama. We must consider the way in which parents and mediators react upon and influence one another; this is not all one-way, with the mediators dictating the course of events and parents responding. This is perhaps most apparent in cases where a parent appears particularly angry (and perhaps threatening) or, conversely, where one parent is very distressed. These two sets of circumstances each create a 'crisis' for the mediators; some will feel relatively comfortable in one situation, but not in another. Parents are likely to assess mediators' competence according to their response to these challenges which they, the parents, have posed in the first place.

This recognition that individual mediators respond differently to a particular set of circumstances has an important practical application: it is an additional argument for having *two* mediators present at each appointment, although, as we shall see, this can also be problematic.

Parents

We must also consider what it is that individual parents bring to the bureau. For example, what is the strength of feeling involved in each case? Are parents willing to negotiate together. Second, we have to ask whether parents feel *able* to talk frankly about these issues. Does either side feel under threat? Do they have the confidence and verbal skills that may be necessary in order to discuss the problem with strangers?

We asked parents how they would describe the tone of the discussion at the bureau. Only four of those interviewed (8 per cent) described the meeting as 'friendly' or 'relaxed'. Seventeen (33 per cent) thought that the conversation had been reserved or strained, or at best 'neutral' in tone, while 30 people (59 per cent) told us that the discussion had been distinctly angry or hostile. Women were rather more likely than men to say that they had found the discussion painful or hostile.

Apart from anything else, these results give the lie to any suggestion that couples who are prepared to attend a mediation appointment must be on a reasonably friendly footing. It is clear that the great majority of these couples were by no means 'friendly'. In many cases this did not preclude an agreement being reached. For example, of the seven bureau 'agreements' amongst cases in which we interviewed both husband and wife, there were three in which they each regarded the discussion as having been acrimonious. Of the other four, at least one parent, and sometimes both, thought that the negotiations had been tense or strained. In other words, these agreements did not flow from relaxed, 'sweetness and light' negotiating sessions. On the contrary, the usual pattern was for there to be a search for specific practical agreements against a background of continuing conflict. In many cases the parents had no desire to improve their relationship with one another. (For comparable findings, based on research in the USA, see Pearson and Thoennes, 1984).

So even where agreement is reached, mediation in family disputes need not reflect a harmonious relationship between the parents. Indeed, it may well not reflect 'positive' feelings at all. The key to it often lies in the parties' capacity to set aside bitterness and anger, at least for the moment. The 'reward' of negotiating some agreement, say in relation to access, has to offset the powerful temptation to continue battling.

At Bromley it emerged in several cases that although the relationship between the parents had been very strained, one of them, if not both, had gone to great lengths to try to rise above this. The eventual agreement had to be attributed as much to parents' ability to negotiate under stress, as it did to the efforts of the mediators. Thus, in the case of Mr and Mrs Dennis, the wife was initially unprepared to make any concessions to her husband because of his behaviour in leaving the family. She regarded the act of his leaving her and their children as 'rendering his commitment null and void . . . he had forfeited any claim to reasonableness by his actions'. Mrs Dennis was also bitter at what she saw as her husband's failure to make adequate financial provision for her. She regarded the access question as comparatively unimportant when set alongside his decision to end the marriage and his subsequent failure to acknowledge the importance of her role as the person responsible for the children's day-to-day care: 'He's quite happy to do anything for *them*, but he's not happy to do anything which involves me, i.e. anything to do with the house or me, or me with them, is a non-event as far as he's concerned and that I get very worked up over.'

Mr Dennis understood and acknowledged his wife's resentment. As he put it: 'I should not be granted the privilege of that convenience [access] because I'd caused. . . . I can't have it all my own way.'

The case of Mr and Mrs Dennis demonstrates that parents don't arrive at the bureau with just one problem (i.e. access) that they want to discuss; they may carry a whole 'baggage' of seething resentments that, even if they are not voiced directly, may effectively scupper the negotiations.

However, even in these apparently unpromising circumstances, something of value may be achieved. In the end, following three appointments, Mr and Mrs Dennis arrived at an access arrangement that was acceptable to them both. Mr Dennis found the whole process exhausting: 'it was difficult, lengthy, tedious'. His wife would not respond to the highly 'rational' way in which he attempted to tackle the problem. This clash of approaches frustrated them both. Indeed, this was one of the more protracted mediation attempts that we came across. Nevertheless, given the resistance that Mrs Dennis brought to the initial appointment, the fact that they made as much progress as they did was remarkable (although it is perhaps not insignificant that Mrs Dennis still thought the 'bargain' went her husband's way in the end).

The case of Mr and Mrs Parks was another in which the mother felt very bitter towards her husband and was initially determined not to grant him access. As with Mrs Dennis, she did in the end abandon this very entrenched position and reconsider her own motives and behaviour. She acknowledged the part which the mediators played in this, but equally, one must recognize the demands placed upon Mrs Parks's own resources:

> We went to the Family Reconciliation Service (*sic*) and they certainly solved the gap at the time. I didn't want him to have access whatsoever, not one ounce, not one iota, and I was so . . . I'd made my decision in my mind. He'd made his choice, another woman. She's got two children. Let him have her and her two kids, you know, he wasn't going to have me or my two kids and I was so on one wavelength and I couldn't see nobody else's point of view . . . and we went to this family reconciliation and they was very good, I must admit. You know, at least I could see when somebody else was telling me it's not fair from his point of view. I then saw it, but until that point I couldn't.

The way in which the mediators seek to persuade parents to shift their ground – and the fact that it may be more often the mother who is called upon to make concessions – are topics we examine in later chapters. For the moment we are concerned only to demonstrate how important it is that the parties have some capacity to negotiate together – which means, above all, that each has to be prepared to reconsider their own position.

It might be thought that the parents' decision to take their quarrel to a mediation agency is itself indicative of a willingness to negotiate. But this is not always the case. Parents may be seeking partisan support, rather than disinterested help; they may not even want to settle the dispute at all, seeking instead a forum in which to air grievances, or a means of demonstrating their own 'reasonableness' prior to a court hearing. Legal anthropologists have much to tell us about the ways in which a mediator may be 'used' by the parties. For example:

> one strategy of a disputant is to accept the intervention of a mediator in the expectation of persuading him of the validity and strength of one's own demands or of the reality of one's commitment to a stand in order to gain his influence upon the opponent. The mediator may become, perhaps unwittingly, a kind of ally.
>
> (Gulliver, 1979, p. 218)

The Bromley bureau is regularly faced with these and other difficulties. Our impression is that most parents are genuinely motivated to seek agreement, but mediators have occasionally suggested to us that some people are 'doing the rounds', having their say to anyone who will listen. Of course, if true, the reasons *why* parents should feel the need to seek additional partisan support in this way are themselves worth exploring. They may, for example, experience a lack of support from their solicitor, or have difficulty in securing a court hearing to decide their case. Others will feel that they have gone past the stage of negotiation, of finding common ground, or of being 'reasonable'. This may reflect the recent marital history – or, in some cases, the changed balance of power brought about through the couple's separation.

In some of the Bromley cases, the woman, perhaps for the first time, appeared to have achieved a relatively powerful position – at least in relation to the access question. But in these circumstances there is no reason to suppose that she should have confidence in her own or anyone else's ability to control the outcome of a negotiation; everything may have to be fought for, with all the limited strength at her disposal. Nor should it be assumed that in pursuing 'negotiation', the husband is genuinely wanting to understand his wife's point of view. He is not uninvolved; some husbands, indeed, are extremely hostile. They may be seeking an opportunity to cast blame, or exert pressure. Certainly this was suspected by some wives.

Whilst only a minority of our Bromley interview sample displayed quite this degree of distance between husband and wife, there were cases in which the parents' antipathy or mutual distrust was very marked and their capacity to negotiate together correspondingly limited. Perhaps the best illustration of this is in the following case where both parents said that they had gained nothing from the bureau, although they blamed each other for this, rather than the mediators. As the wife put it:

They did try, they tried very hard, the woman especially. But it was a real slanging match, we were both screaming at each other. The young lady tried very hard to calm us down but she couldn't manage it. I think it depends on who they are seeing. It'd probably work with most people, but it didn't work with me and my husband.

The husband, so he said, had entertained some hopes of a reconciliation at this stage, but for a man seeking to mend his marriage, he had a rather low opinion of his wife:

I mean, my wife was a liar. I went along just to keep the peace. My wife is a liar, always will be a liar, and I wouldn't trust her. I mean, I had her back here three times and I used to think, oh, she's back, OK, we're going to be happy. Ten minutes later I wish she hadn't bloody well come. . . . Once a liar, always a liar – God help me, the excuses I've had to make for my wife.

Neither party could be said to have brought a self-critical approach to their marital problems, but equally, it would be quite wrong to assume that this couple *ought* to have been able to negotiate a way out of their difficulties. Given their respect-ive temperaments and the situation they were in, negotiation was probably not appropriate. As the husband explained, 'we only reached one conclusion – agree to disagree'. The only consolation – and it is a fairly limited one – is that the visit to the bureau did not appear to have made their situation worse.

7

Mediators' use of authority

One of the key objectives underlying the offer of mediation in
family disputes is that control over decision-making should, as
far as possible, remain with the parties themselves. *The
mediators' authority derives from them.* This is a point many
social workers and divorce court welfare officers find difficult to
grasp. It is understandable that they should be interested in
'conciliation'; many of the aspirations and values with which
this term is now identified are consistent with social work's
own body of theory and range of approaches, for example, with
'short-term working' and a non-judgemental stance. But the
concept of 'party-control' remains stubbornly incompatible
with key elements within the social work (and divorce court
welfare) tradition. This is because social workers and welfare
officers have to balance their clients' wishes against the con-
straints imposed by agency responsibilities (such as taking
children into care). They are used to *holding* authority, rather
than ensuring that this is retained by parents. Mediators, on the
other hand, are invited by parents to contribute to the negotiation process. They have no authority to decide the outcome.
To the extent that one or both parents may appear to want the

mediators to take on this arbitrating role, the offer should be declined.

The Central Council of Probation and After-Care Committees (which includes the divorce court welfare service within its area of responsibility) has evidently failed to recognize the limited nature of mediator authority when it suggests that '[t]here is clearly a connection between the work of probation officers in domestic conciliation and their work with offenders who are in conflict not only with their families but also with society'.[1]

Unfortunately, to equate 'conciliation' in family disputes (where the mediator has a purely facilitating role) with 'conciliation' between offender and state only serves to demonstrate the paternalistic assumptions by means of which the Probation Service could distort the mediation concept. Separating parents who bring their quarrel to a mediator remain free agents. One or both may feel in a very weak position, but at the mediation stage they have lost nothing. This changes, of course, as soon as a court is involved. But the object of mediation is to help parents avoid the need for such loss of authority.

But in practice the lack of formal authority need not preclude a directive approach. There were a few cases in which the Bromley mediators gave every appearance of assuming decision-making power, presumably on the basis that their expert knowledge made this desirable. It is often tempting to claim special knowledge and, particularly in relation to access, trained social workers (as are some of the Bromley mediators) may well feel that they know what the best outcome would be from the child's point of view. 'Client self-determination' is a slippery concept at the best of times and McDermott (1975, p. 124) has described how, in social work usage, 'the laudatory force of the expression . . . is deflected from the rather disturbing idea of the client doing what he wants to, on to the altogether more congenial notion of his doing what is prudent, rational, moral, and in every way praiseworthy'.

It is fair to say, however, that the bulk of the evidence from parents interviewed at Bromley is reassuring on this point. They felt that responsibility for decisions taken did indeed rest with them. In a few instances, they had been disappointed and perhaps rather disconcerted that this was so. The following comment from one of the men we interviewed provides a clear illustration of this:

> I understood the meaning of the word 'conciliation' so I already had this idea of what they were going to try and achieve. I came out thinking 'Well, I must have got it wrong'. . . . I thought they'd have a bit more power. And it wasn't until I was in there that I realized that they were just there for guidance.

Mr Selvey was another non-custodial parent who was disappointed to discover that the mediator (there appears to have been only one in his case) lacked decision-making power and therefore could not provide a remedy for the weakness of his position relative to that of his former wife:

> You see, what happens is, isn't it, people, they go back and others say 'I wouldn't have that. Don't do that. You don't have to agree to that – oh, bugger them, they don't count for anything, or they don't make any difference at all, you know. You sort out what you want and the court will uphold that. You're the main parent, you know. The child's at your place', and all the rest of it . . . and then they [custodial parents] just kind of, instead of feeling sensitive to their own responsibilities, they can hide behind what others have done and what the status quo is, what the norm is.

Mr Selvey also came to recognize that the bureau was not like the divorce court welfare service, influencing the court; if anything, this 'influence' operated in the other direction: the norms the mediators tried to uphold were in line with precedents set by the courts when adjudicating similar disputes:

> It's the courts that determine those norms. All the rest of it, including the conciliation bureau, is determined ultimately by what the courts do. It's not that the bureau informs the courts in a way that influences the court's decisions. No, it's not that. That's my experience. It's the other way round. It's the bureau are governed by what they think the court are prepared to insist on or accept or uphold.

Mr Selvey's arguments are interesting (and potentially confusing) because when he talks of the mediator's authority, or influence, he is using these terms in two different ways. Perhaps this will become clear on reading the next extract:

> I think they are capable of having more influence on the outcome of decisions than they do have. That's to say that the co-mixture of advice, guidance and direction that it's essential for them to give enables them to have a position of responsibility and a certain position of influence that they must use in the best interests of the children and the best interests of the couple. And not to be so laid back and sort of California dreaming that, you know, people come in there, they wander about and they think, well, this is some mild therapy session. It doesn't lead anywhere.

We have to draw a distinction between, on the one hand, authority to determine the outcome of the negotiation, and on the other, the mediator's ability to influence the negotiation *process*, drawing on the authority to facilitate which is vested in him by parents. Mr Selvey had been hoping that the mediator would be more directive, to the point where he would decide the outcome and then draw on the authority of the court in order to enforce his decision. In that respect, the bureau was bound to be a disappointment to him.

But in addition, Mr Selvey felt that the mediator should have assumed a more active role in the discussion, saying what he believed and challenging parents if he felt that they were being unreasonable or inconsistent. This is a different notion of 'authority' and one that is not, in itself, at odds with a mediating role:

> The moment she started taking up an unreasonable line, [mediator] backed away. He wouldn't say 'Well, that's a bit unreasonable, J, isn't it?', you know. 'What you said before was so and so.' And then he lost his authority as a negotiator because instead of being consistent within the terms of reference he'd used previously and the criteria he was employing, as a counsellor, as a concerned person, as a, you know, probation officer and all the rest of it, he was seen to be more concerned with not stepping on her toes or up-

setting her or not having any particular point of view. And
of course, the whole thing just dissipated. Any sense of
objective authority that might have been represented there
just sort of faded away. And that was it. That was the
opportunity lost . . . he was too pussyfooting. He was, for
whatever reason, so concerned to be seen as some kind of
. . . I suppose . . . detached and impartial, almost observer,
that there wasn't a sense of solid purpose about him.

The question that has to be considered here is whether Mr
Selvey was seeking a more active and dynamic form of intervention than the mediator in his case was prepared to offer, or
whether, in reality, he wanted him to take on an arbitrating role
in order to persuade his wife that she was in the wrong and
should therefore give way. The expectation that the mediator be
prepared to comment on either party's stance in the course of
the discussion strikes us as perfectly reasonable, although much
depends on how this is done. On the other hand, it would appear
that Mr Selvey was hoping that the mediator would use his
professional status as court welfare officer in order to bring
pressure to bear on his wife. There is reason to be sceptical as to
whether such an approach, had it been adopted, would have had
much influence on Mrs Selvey, because this is what she had to
say:

> *Mrs Selvey:* I didn't know at the time that he was a welfare
> officer . . . I didn't know that till some time later. In fact,
> I'm glad I didn't know it at the time because I might have
> been more inhibited if I had. He didn't let that come into it
> at all. He didn't give me the impression that he had any
> power or that he would use any power. He was simply
> trying to be helpful.
> *Interviewer:* It was probably in a different capacity that
> he was seeing you?
> *Mrs Selvey:* Yes, that's right. But not everybody could
> have separated one from the other. He was able to. I have
> great admiration for [mediator].

What makes this case particularly interesting is that Mrs
Selvey picks up the same point as her husband, namely that the
mediator, whilst he occupied a position of formal authority in

his role as court welfare officer, had divested himself of that status for the purpose of mediation; he was not prepared to bring pressure to bear on either party. Unlike her husband, Mrs Selvey regarded the two appointments at the bureau as a useful experience, even though no agreement was reached.

It is possible to infer from Mr Selvey's account that when he said that he would have liked the mediator to show greater authority, he was assuming that this would be exercised to his advantage. Perhaps underlying his remarks is a suspicion that the mediator had indeed been 'recruited' – but by his wife. Indeed, some of Mrs Selvey's other comments suggest that she herself recognized that the mediator's sympathies lay with her rather than with her husband. (She picked this up through the mediator's non-verbal behaviour, something which Mr Selvey may also have noted, although he did not comment on it.)

The case of Mr and Mrs Dennis also serves to illuminate parents' views as to the nature of the mediators' authority. In this instance, the husband claimed that his wife was wanting the mediators to tell her what form of access arrangements she should be prepared to enter into:

> She says that . . . I must try and get this right . . . she doesn't know what's right for the children. And she's not going to take any decision unless she does know what's right. And I've had to point out that she's taking a decision by *not* allowing them to come. But actually – I mean, I can't get that across and that's why, interestingly enough, I see her thinking of the conciliation service as an arbitration service. She expects somebody else to decide what's right. What's right for two individuals she thinks somebody else can decide in a way that will absolve her from the difficulty, which I recognize, of moving along a path that she doesn't want to travel. But she does expect it to be laid down.

Whilst the mediators in this case did not tell these parents what they ought to do, it is clear that they exercised considerable influence upon the negotiation. Mrs Dennis's account gives us the best indication so far of the way in which the mediators can achieve this, without undermining parents' authority. The change effected in this case was all the more remarkable given the resistance Mrs Dennis acknowledged she brought to the bureau:

> I will tell you quite frankly, I went to that meeting and I was prepared to sit there and say nothing. I felt there was nothing for me to say; everybody knew what the situation was. My case had been stated. The onus was on my husband to convince them or to convince me or whichever it went, that he had a gripe. And so I must admit I probably sat there for, if you can believe this, for about three-quarters of an hour being really very monosyllabic and almost detached. And then various aspects started to be . . . [mediator], I must admit he was very . . . I was quite amazed at this man – his ability to say nothing, yet say a lot. He somehow started to draw me out and slowly things started to be talked about, not the issue, but the ramifications to the issue, which really had been bottled up in me so long because whenever I tried to talk these out with Michael [husband] he never ever listened. He maintained *I* never listened, but equally he, you know, never listened either.

The key points to note here are, first, that the mediators encouraged the parents to talk – to the point where, in the end, they were able to say things to one another they had not been able to manage on their own; and second, in doing so, they did not only focus on the access question – in this case, whether the children should stay with their father overnight – but they gave time to exploring the mother's underlying resentments, these having clearly influenced her approach to access.

In summing up the mediators' conduct of this appointment, it is striking that both husband and wife use the same language. First, Mr Dennis: 'They were very clear in putting the onus on the individuals. They couldn't achieve what individuals didn't want themselves to achieve. They were if you like the catalysts, the vehicle for change without themselves being able to effect any change.' Mrs Dennis: 'They don't say a lot, do they really? It's the parties who say things, isn't it? And the conciliators are really there as a sort of catalyst, aren't they?'

Mr and Mrs Parks provide another example of the mediators' refusal to adopt a directive stance. However, in this instance both parents felt that the mediators were prepared to do what Mr Selvey had complained was *not* done in his case, namely, to express a point of view. They seem to have made a number of comments about the way in which each parent approached the negotiation, but apparently they managed this in such a way that the message was acceptable. As Mr Parks described it:

It was very good, I must admit. I was a bit apprehensive 'cos I thought here we go . . . you've got to sit there and talk to a bloke . . . don't know what he's talking about. I was surprised, I must admit, I was very surprised. He was very good. Made you see a lot of faults in yourself. He sort of made me look an idiot because I'm very funny on punctuality – he sort of made me look at myself from outside, sort of thing. As I say, I found it very, very good.

To make someone look at himself 'from outside', even to make him 'look an idiot', apparently without causing resentment, bears testimony to the skills of the mediators in this case. Mrs Parks's comments were similar:

They had the patience of a saint. They were very patient and they were very understanding, because I don't think you need somebody to sit and tell you what to do and how to do it and anything like that, because at that point you're not ready for it – but somebody who is willing to give advice, 'Well, I think this is going wrong and that is going wrong', you can accept that. But I can't be told by anybody what to do, you know. They was very good. They didn't say 'do this' and 'do that', but they put it in such a way that you could accept it.

There are certain types of problem that bring out a little more clearly the possible conflict between the mediators' wish to be non-directive and the temptation for them to give parents the benefit of their own views. This dilemma is a reflection of the tension, inherent in the mediator's role, between the goal of settling a dispute and the lack of power to impose a decision (Silbey and Merry, 1986). The mediators nevertheless have considerable opportunity to influence *the process* whereby a

decision will be reached. They may also, as in the case of Mr
Todd, give advice:

> I was given a certain amount of advice actually, along the
> lines that they felt that if I continued to see Clare [child]
> she would still be put under pressure at home. They felt
> that my ex-wife would still pressure her and so forth and
> they didn't think that that would change. They said, I seem
> to remember, that it would be very nice if she [ex-wife]
> would take the view that I'm not going to do anything to
> disrupt their home life, but they felt she couldn't do that
> and therefore it would be kindest for me just not to put the
> child into a situation where she was going to be pressured.

In this case the mediators were unable to reconcile the
parents' conflicting views as to whether access to the father was
in the child's interests. They pointed out the possible implications of various courses of action and in the end Mr Todd
came to the view that he should give up access to the elder girl
altogether. On the face of it, this is a rather surprising line for the
mediators to take – and perhaps it is even more surprising that
Mr Todd went along with it. But it appears that he was genuinely persuaded that continued access would undermine his
daughter's happiness. Second, his willingness to accept the mediators' assessment becomes a little more understandable when
one hears what he had to say about other views they expressed,
since these appeared to support his side of the argument:

> The business of Val and Alan [ex-wife and step-parent]
> wanting to change the children's surname was something
> which came up and I remember she was told you can't take
> the children's identity away like this. You mustn't suggest
> it to them. It's not the sort of thing one should do.

One important function of third-party mediation is to provide
an opportunity for graceful retreat, or face-saving (Pruitt and
Johnson, 1970). The Bromley mediators often go to considerable
lengths to bolster the parent (usually the custodian, and therefore usually the mother) who is being asked to make the tangible
concessions. This is a point we address in the context of men
and women's different experiences of mediation, since it often
seemed that the custodial mother was being asked to give

ground, she meantime receiving considerable support from the
mediators in order to help her do this. But in this instance it was
the man who ended up making a very substantial sacrifice. At
the same time, Mr Todd was reassured by the mediators as far as
possible, and confirmed in his position as the children's father: 'I
think the biggest thing that came across, other than the two
main agreements, was that Val [ex-wife] was made aware of the
fact that I am the children's father and nothing she or anybody
else can do can change that. She shouldn't try to.'

Mr Todd's account hardly gives the impression of 'lack of
solid purpose' or of the 'pussyfooting' to which Mr Selvey had
referred. These mediators seemed all too ready to advise the
parents about the decisions they should make in their children's
interests, given that they could not agree. But they seem to have
managed this in a way that, to Mr Todd at least, appears to have
been even-handed. What is more, he was clear that, ultimately,
the decision was his:

> I think the beauty of it was, they let you make your own
> decisions. They weren't forcing their opinions on you.
> They were just giving you another side of an argument
> perhaps. They were exposing the whole thing so you could
> look at it logically. I think if there were any pressure at all,
> the pressure was . . . you have to consider what's best for
> the children. And that wasn't done in a nasty way. It was
> done very gently really. They certainly let us come to our
> own decision. And at the end of the day they said, 'yes,
> that sounds reasonable to us'. I get the feeling that if they
> hadn't considered it reasonable, they would have said
> so.

It is apparent from these accounts that the mediators have
their own values and are prepared to express these. Some succeed in doing this with considerable subtlety, so that it appears
that they are exerting no influence at all; others express their
ideas so gently and with such obvious concern that the parents
themselves not be offended by them, that their suggestions tend
to be accepted. In many of these cases there was an obvious
identity of values between the mediators and the parents.

We asked all parents who reached agreement at the bureau
whether they had felt under pressure from the mediators. Of the

32 who reported that an agreement had been reached, 9 (28 per cent) said that they had been put under pressure. It is interesting, given the suggestion that women, being predominantly custodial parents, are more likely to be required to give ground on the access question, that only 2 of the 14 women who reported an agreement (14 per cent) said they had been put under pressure, as against 7 of the 18 men (39 per cent). This is something to be weighed in the balance in Chapter 11, where we consider the differential impact of mediation on men and women.

Rather than complain about being pressurized by the mediators, several parents interviewed at Bromley expressed the view that mediation by its very nature contributes to an expectation that there be some compromise, or at least that parents shift from their original positions. For example, this is how one mother replied to our question about pressure: 'No, there wasn't. There was a pressure to accept something and to make a compromise, for both of us to make a compromise because obviously neither of us were going to come to perfect agreement, otherwise we wouldn't have been there in the first place.'

The very fact that these parents had sought third-party help placed them in a position where they were expected to find a solution. Also, parents will want to look good in the eyes of the mediators, which means that they will want to appear as reasonable as possible. This is a well-established feature of mediation in any setting (Rubin and Brown, 1975, p. 56) and may be distinguished from the kind of pressurizing tactics employed in negotiation on court premises (Davis and Bader, 1985), or, in some instances, in the course of a welfare enquiry (Davis, 1988). This was how a father in a different case developed this same point:

> Conciliation shouldn't really be about exercising pressure, should it? It's about talking. . . . nevertheless, one feels obliged to come to an agreement because maybe there are people looking at you in a way, saying 'Now come on, be reasonable. Maybe there's a compromise. Maybe there's a solution. We can't go on behaving like this with this situation. . . .' That in itself, the whole situation exercises pressure.

For the most part, the Bromley mediators succeed in conveying to parents that it is their judgements and views of the quarrel that matter, while nevertheless demonstrating an unobtrusive capacity to guide them in the direction of one, or perhaps several possible solutions.

Note

1 Central Council of Probation and After-Care Committees (1983) *Submission to the Inter-departmental Committee on Conciliation*, Unpublished.

8

Judgement and interpretation

It has been pointed out by several writers that, whatever the area of conflict, mediators will tend to have their own interests, values and perceptions that need not coincide with those of the disputants (Gulliver, 1979, p. 214 f.). At Bromley, we have seen how the mediators' own values play a part in shaping the discussion and in guiding parents towards what they, the mediators, deem to be suitable options. We have also noted that sensitively proffered advice from the mediators appears to be acceptable, whereas most parents have a strong resistance to being judged or blamed.

There were a few accounts that suggested that the mediators had indeed dominated the proceedings. The result was that parents saw themselves as the subject of judgement on the one hand, or of 'treatment' on the other. In these circumstances it was the mediators' perception of the problem that had predominated, this being afforded a kind of scientific authority. Far from impressing parents, as was presumably the intention, this approach was often regarded as inappropriate and false. This was the view of one custodial father:

They seemed too authoritarian about it all and this was when I first started getting the smack of the, well, look, you know, we've got the textbooks here and this is how you do it, and you do this and you do that and it's written here and we had a case last week . . . it was too scientific. They had a theory and this was their theory. They probably had a preconceived theory before you'd even walked into their office. In other words, they weren't prepared to start from scratch with two new people's problems.

This criticism parallels that made of some solicitors at the point when they were first consulted about a matrimonial problem, it being suggested that they were too quick to 'pigeon-hole' issues in order that they might apply their technical expertise. This meant that complex problems were re-defined to fit *their* categories, rather than being expressed in ways that made sense to the client.

However, there are differences between solicitors and mediators in this respect. The kind of 're-defining' solicitors feel bound to undertake because of pressure of time or the need to fit a given problem within the legal framework is of a different order to the categorization of problems that is employed by some mediators. The latter appears to arise from a view that it is necessary to warn parents of the damage being inflicted on children through parental quarrelling, or the loss of all contact with the non-custodial parent. Reference may be made to 'research' that is supportive of these views. But parents complained that they didn't need to be told those things; they felt just as strongly about them as did the mediators. As one mother explained:

I'm sure they're very helpful people, but me, the person I am, I know that [about children needing to see their father] – that is something I know. I know more about family life than many people – it's something I desperately want in my whole life, even now. So for me, that didn't particularly apply.

In a few instances the mediators were seen to be putting their own interpretive gloss on the proceedings, making psychological judgements and getting them wrong. The following non-custodial father complained that the mediators had commented on his past relationship with his wife, thereby straying into irrelevant domains:

> *Father*: She [mediator] said something which I wasn't quite happy about. She said that I hadn't quite given her up. I hadn't quite given my wife up, you know. I hadn't let go. That wasn't an issue – it wasn't one of the issues involved.
> *Interviewer*: You didn't think that was a fair remark?
> *Father*: No, I didn't think so.

It may be that in some cases the mediators feel driven to be more interpretive than they would wish as a result of what they fear may be problems of control arising in the mediation session. Mr and Mrs Bennett provide perhaps the best example of this. Mr Bennett is a big man who, certainly on first impression, appears quite a dominating character. Perhaps because he felt that he needed to protect Mrs Bennett, one mediator made some quite critical judgements about him that he found hurtful and that led him to believe that his own problems were not appreciated:

> I felt at one stage he [mediator] was coming across a bit strong. I mean, maybe it wasn't intentional, but he seemed to be inferring things that weren't happening. I mean, he was saying to me that I was headstrong and ... I can't remember details ... but I mean he was just implying things. I thought, taking into consideration that he was supposed to be just there to keep the peace, more or less, and to listen and to help us sort things out, he was chipping in more than that. He was trying to tell me what to say to my wife, how I should be with my wife. And like, I dunno, we had words.

We suspect that there are certain personal characteristics – not necessarily virtues in another context – that may help to counteract any tendency for the mediator to express judgements of this kind. Mediators need to be tolerant people, without too many strong opinions about what constitutes right behaviour. They should be like Mr Brooke of Middlemarch, a man who had his limitations in many respects, but who had long held that 'it is a narrow mind which cannot look at a subject from various points of view'.

Unfortunately, there were other aspects of Mr Brooke's character which suggest that, as a mediator, he would have been disastrously ill-equipped. A kindly disposition and benevolent view of one's fellow men and women is not enough in itself. The mediating role sometimes calls for a willingness to challenge powerful personalities with strongly held views. Nevertheless, it is as well to remember that the mediator is, above all, a *facilitator*. The skills demanded in this respect are not so much a theoretical knowledge of child development, as the ability to stimulate communication and provide a non-threatening framework within which parents may explore their differences and discuss options in a way they would not have been able to do if left to their own devices.

This leads us to be wary of attempts on the part of social work and 'therapeutic' professionals to appropriate mediation (see, for example, James and Wilson, 1986, p. 201), although we recognize that certain of the skills associated with social work are extremely helpful. These include possessing some 'feel' for power imbalances; an ability to recognize when parents are under stress; and third, being attuned to the possibility that silence, or apparent acquiescence, need not indicate genuine consent. These are areas in which social workers *ought* to be better equipped than lawyers[1] and from these parents' accounts it would appear that some, at least, of the Bromley mediators possess these skills to a very high degree. As Mr Parks recalled:

> Yes, they were very understanding. They obviously knew that what you was trying to do was obviously for the best for the kids and all you wanted to do was have your parental rights. I think they tried to do it in such a way that they didn't cause arguments. They was very, very clever the way they put questions as well, you know . . . that way you could sort of get things off your chest without actually upsetting her or causing a row.

Mr Parks felt that he and his wife shared a private language, but he considered, nevertheless, that the mediators had succeeded in overcoming this. Indeed, he suggested that a key distinction between mediation and negotiation alongside solicitors was that mediators were better equipped to break down these barriers:

> I think at the moment me and my ex-wife have got a sort of certain code of talking and we know now what we can talk about and what we can't talk about, you know, what to say and what not to say. I think with solicitors they might say the wrong thing and start rows.

In a few cases there appeared to have been a kind of unspoken understanding between the parents that some personal details should not be revealed. Mr Bennett, for example, reckoned that the mediators would always be denied access to very sensitive information (such as Mrs Bennett's lesbian relationship, in his own case):

> No matter how much you talk about why your marriage broke down and all the rest of it, there are still things that your wife or you and your partner won't discuss, I mean that are personal, and it's them things the conciliation bureau couldn't help with. And they're the things that are important.

Another problem faced by the mediators is that of getting on the same wavelength as parents in the course of one interview. It was not only Mr Parks who referred to a kind of private 'code' that had been learnt by the couple, so that even though they were no longer intimate, this understanding persisted and defied penetration by outsiders. A father in a different case made the same point:

> Two people that have lived together for years and know each other incredibly well, both know by an expression or a gesture or a sentence what the other one is saying, whilst the two people that are interviewing you, don't. So something that's annoying you, they may not even know about.

Despite this apparently pessimistic comment, the father quoted here was full of praise for the female mediator's sensitivity and understanding. It may well be true, as he implies, that there remains a subterranean area of the dispute that is barred to even the most sympathetic outsider, but this does not mean that nothing of value can be achieved.

Mediators' knowledge of the family

Other parents complained that the mediators were ignorant of certain key aspects of the family history, although there is clearly a limit to what mediation can be expected to offer in this respect. To assert that the mediators need to have an understanding of the family background might lead one to ask, Whose *version* of that history are they expected to familiarize themselves with? It has been suggested (Bernard, 1982) that there are two marriages in every marital union, the man's and the woman's. In many instances their two accounts cannot easily be reconciled, in which case the mediator is at risk of being pushed into an arbitrating role.

It might be argued, on the other hand, that this is to posit a situation in which mediation is unlikely to be successful in any event. There has to be some common ground between the parties in the way in which they view the recent history of the dispute if the negotiation is to have any hope of success. Given this limited degree of congruence, it appears that the Bromley mediators *are* prepared to listen and to be influenced by the parties' accounts of the history of their relationship. In the case of Mr Rice and Ms Harvey, the mother felt that the mediators' general stance was supportive of her position, partly because of the responsibilities she bore as the custodial parent, and partly because they took into account the father's record of violence towards her, something he himself did not deny:

> Well, I think it was this thing that the woman looks after the child and so his point of view was less important as regards how often he saw her in that I would obviously be having care of her. But given his history, his record, quite frankly I don't blame them for taking that sort of view 'cos he is really violent – not with her at all, he'd never touch her, but he was very violent with me – which obviously, I mean, that was part of the relationship. So there was a certain bias in that direction.

It might be argued that since the mediators' task (as we have presented it) is to help the parents arrive at agreed decisions, it really does not much matter what they know and don't know; they are facilitators, not arbitrators. Such a view fails to take account of the considerable degree of authority most parents are prepared to vest in the mediators. Parents are the key decision-makers and it is vital that they accept the terms of any agreement; but there is an expectation on all sides that the mediators will play an active part in the search for settlement. This exerts pressure of a kind, so that parents are right to feel that the mediators' understanding of the conflict will affect the outcome. This is not to deny the 'party-control' that is at the heart of the mediation idea; but it is to acknowledge the reality that this may be tempered by third-party influence and moral pressure.

Mediators' level of understanding

There is also the question of whether parents thought that the mediators had sufficient life experience, or imagination, to enable them to understand the problem as parents experienced it. Thirty of the Bromley parents (59 per cent) felt the mediators had been able to do this, whilst 18 (35 per cent) said that they had not. One parent was 'uncertain' and the other two distinguished between the mediators in this respect, considering that one of them had been able to understand, while the other had not. It is interesting to note that of the small group of five custodial fathers, only one said that he thought that the mediators had understood the difficulties he faced.

Several parents were aware (or suspected) that the mediators had had no personal experience of divorce. They felt that this contributed to a lack of understanding. In the words of one non-custodial father:

> This is something I've often wondered, that perhaps it's wrong of me to say in a way, that the sort of person who was interviewing me I couldn't imagine could ever have been in my position. I think that is one thing I do remember about the interview. I mean . . . I just took it that that's their job and they are qualified . . . but they couldn't really understand it first-hand.

It is fair to say that the wife in this case considered that the distress involved was by its nature incommunicable; she did not blame the mediators' lack of experience or imagination.

Another criticism was that the mediators (one, if not both)

had been too young. The woman quoted below claimed that the appointment had been 'a waste of time'. The access arrangement she and her husband eventually arrived at was made *after* the meeting at the bureau, as they walked to the bus-stop together. Of the mediators, she had this to say:

> I remember thinking how young they were, well, the boy. And I thought, well, he's a bit young, you know. I always think people that do that sort of work should have had the experience of perhaps living through something like that themselves. But he seemed so young. I think there was a much older lady. They were very friendly. They were very nice. But as I say, I didn't think I got over to them what I was trying to say.

This criticism that the mediators had lacked direct experience is, of course, one to which almost anyone who intervenes in other people's relationship difficulties might be thought vulnerable. The point was made again and again in the course of a parallel investigation of divorce court welfare practice, conducted in Bristol (Davis, forthcoming). We suspect, in fact, that it matters little whether the mediator is young, or for that matter unmarried. Some descriptions we came across (such as 'spinster' or 'boy') may be seen as convenient labels to be applied to those mediators (or welfare officers) who convey through their general approach to the task that they lack experience, or wisdom, or common-sense. Whilst it may be of *some* help if mediators have themselves undergone the pain of separation and divorce, a more important requirement is that they display the kind of concern and imaginative understanding that is necessary if they are to come to terms with other people's problems.

Note

1 This point was made by Wendy Pachter at a symposium held at Vermont Law School in September 1983. A record of these proceedings was disseminated under the title *A Study of Barriers to the Use of Alternative Methods of Dispute Resolution*, Vermont Law School, South Royalton, Vermont, 1984.

9

Controlling the exchanges

Any close relationship, if it is to endure, demands continued negotiation. Those involved need not be verbally sophisticated, but there still has to be negotiation of a kind. Married couples, like colleagues at work, have to find some way of getting along and this involves having to recognize one another's point of view. This may be called 'bringing him down to earth' or 'getting her to see it my way'. It may be in the form of a more or less reasoned discussion, or it could be a blazing row. But in some way, a degree of mutual understanding has to be achieved, although this is very far from saying that the parties will be in accord.

At the time of marital breakdown and separation, there may be no incentive to struggle to sustain even limited communication. It may be difficult for either party to take account of anything beyond the justice of their own position and their spouse's undeniable ability to inflict damage upon them. This can be exacerbated by the legal process, for example, through divorce petitions based on 'unreasonable behaviour' or, more generally, through the lack of direct communication that is characteristic of legal proceedings.

Once this gulf has been established, any attempt to re-open communication between the parties is likely to encounter problems of control. If a mediator is involved, he or she will have to ensure that the couple engage in a discussion that is relatively calm and not simply a point-scoring exercise. This is not to suggest that he or she should attempt to block all expression of feeling. Mediators have to be able to engage in, and indeed may need to encourage, plain speaking. Attempts to 'damp down' or 'smooth over' conflict can only hinder mutual recognition and acknowledgement and so frustrate the whole exercise.

One of the most delicate tasks facing the mediator is that of deciding when (and how) to divert the parties from an exchange that threatens to go past the point of being helpful or cathartic, so leaving them worse off than when they started. The mediator cannot allow this emotional charge to overwhelm and dominate the proceedings. The parties can no doubt achieve that kind of confrontation without his or her help. As one Bromley mediator put it, 'They have to learn to talk again without the rubbish'.

Equally, it has to be understood that this 'rubbish' is not an irrelevant detritus, extraneous to the problem. These emotional tangles may well be what caused the difficulty in the first place. They also provide the basis for the negotiations that follow. The relative points scored and lost by the parties may be part of the process whereby justice is seen to be rendered. Indeed, one of the important things about point-scoring is that, if controlled, it can encourage the notion of exchange: 'You get a point – so now you have to give up a point.'

To regard mediation, where it is effective, as rooted in the parties' sense of fairness is, we believe, more accurate than the emphasis placed by some commentators upon the mediator's symbolic authority.[1] This is because a mediator, unlike the judge in a courtroom, has to rely upon the parties' commitment to a collaborative exercise. As Chapter 6 suggests, this foundation may appear shaky at times, but equally, parents' willingness to attend a joint meeting must be regarded as significant. They cannot be immune to the values that are reflected in a decision to engage in this form of negotiation – values of parental autonomy, shared responsibility and mutual exchange.

This does not mean that the Bromley mediators have an easy task (and of course they cannot rely on the formal trappings of the courtroom to create a mood of awe amongst the participants) but at least they are not alone in their commitment to an ordered discussion. Several parents told us how much they had welcomed the fact that the exchanges at the bureau were reasonably controlled. We were often told that the couple had tried to talk together without a third party being present, but had failed to do so, perhaps because the discussion generated into a 'row' – and a fairly predictable row at that, involving the exchange of ritual accusations. As Mrs Parks explained, 'You know, we're both very private people and the fact that there was another man and another woman in the room, we could sit and discuss things that we couldn't at home. Because every time we tried at home there was fights and rows.'

Mr Parks also recognized that the mediators had enabled him and his wife to communicate in a way they wouldn't have been able to manage on their own. They provided a controlling influence on what had hitherto been uncontrollable exchanges:

> At the beginning, obviously there was things I didn't want Laura [wife] to know about. By the end, well half way through the meeting, I think [mediator] had sort of put you in the position where you had to tell the truth. I think because actually he was sitting there, you could say the truth, and I didn't mind. I found it a lot easier to get off my chest and . . . I mean now I'm still frightened to tell Laura things because obviously when you're on your own, she sort of tends to fly off the handle. He enabled us to talk.

Mr and Mrs Robb were another couple whose case illustrates the importance (to the wife in particular, in this instance) of the mediators exerting firm control over the proceedings. As was the case with Mr and Mrs Bennett, Mrs Robb had felt dominated and rather overwhelmed by her husband, but in the mediators' presence there was no need to resort to the kind of defensive behaviour that would otherwise have been necessary when faced with such a strong character:

> It was sort of like being talked to a bit like a teenager really, but I accepted that. That's part of their job, you know. They

were very stern. They made it clear that they were going to take no nonsense. This wasn't a place for us to argue and threaten and so on, which again I was grateful for because he's a very powerful man and a very, very strong personality and I would've been undermined and my only resource would've been to become extremely angry and I would've been so ashamed afterwards.

Notwithstanding the fact that Mrs Robb thought she and her husband were talked to like teenagers, she was enabled to retain her dignity. She had been badly hurt by her husband's departure and it was very important to her that she prove to him that she was able to engage in a sensible discussion about the future. The mediators enabled her to achieve this:

I felt that at least he could see that I wasn't crumbling to a nothing, that I wasn't so devastated that I couldn't pick myself up by my bootstrings and say, 'Our daughter matters'. I felt that I showed him, by behaving very well, by being very quiet and talking directly and sensibly in front of him that I was prepared to discuss Meg [daughter] and his access to her and her access to him, with professional people. . . . You can talk till kingdom-come over a cup of coffee with friends, mates and so on – what they've been through and their experiences, but I don't think that is very helpful in the long run. You want somebody who is trained . . . more was done in that one interview than in all the talk and shouting, heart searching and crying over telephones and crying in friends' houses and friends coming here . . . 'oh, what'll I do? What *will* I do?' – and all this sort of thing. This was practical.

Mrs Robb was not the only parent we interviewed who equated professionalism with the mediators' ability to control the proceedings and ensure that the weaker party to the dispute was adequately protected. However, Mr Robb, in one of the more divergent assessments we encountered, explicitly denied the mediators' professional competence: 'I thought they were untrained. I thought they were, well . . . to put it kindly, amateurish. . . . I thought my neighbours could have done as well.'

The nature of the conflict in many of these cases, coupled with parents' need to gain support for their own position, meant that their views of the mediators did sometimes differ quite sharply. Nevertheless, there was a degree of congruence when it came to parents' accounts of how the mediators managed to achieve control over the discussion. Some evidently did this in a very formal way and it was interesting to find that this very firm grip on the proceedings was regarded by some parents as evidence in itself of a 'professional' approach:

> I was very surprised at how professional and formal it was. I don't know why. . . . I expected it to be more informal. . . . I would've preferred it to have been more informal from a relaxation point of view. I would've been more relaxed. But they did give the air of being true professionals.

The clearest illustration of some mediators' tendency to achieve 'control' in a rather hectoring, authoritarian fashion came in the case of a couple who were eventually reconciled, although not as a direct result of mediation. The mother had felt rather cowed and inhibited by the mediators:

> He [mediator] stopped that [squabbles] immediately. He said you're here to discuss domestic issues, things what you're going to get settled. You're not here to have petty squabbles over what trousers he should wear and what skirt you should wear and what the kids should wear and all this sort of thing. He said you're here to settle your domestic issues and that's it. And if you're not prepared to do that, you'll have to leave.

But whereas the above accounts and, to a lesser extent, that of Mrs Robb suggest that in order to achieve control over the proceedings, some mediators 'talk down' to parents, other mediators seemed to intervene in a much less obtrusive fashion. They were accessible and low key, rather than formidable. Mr Parks's account gives the impression of a relaxed 'facilitator' rather than of a boxing referee keeping a warring couple apart through a strict application of the Queensberry Rules:

> I'll be quite honest. When we went to see – I can't think of his name; —, I think it was – we found him very, very . . .

oh, he was fantastic. I couldn't praise that bloke enough.
Well, we went there – it was purely for the access of the
children – and I think he done more, I think if . . . how can I
put it? . . . if things had been a little bit different when we
got home, I'll be quite honest, I don't think the marriage
would've split up. He done that good of a job of talking to
us. He made things make more sense, you know – it was
very good indeed. You know, I'd commend that bloke to
anybody. He was fantastic, he was. You know, he made us
feel very, very at ease and very friendly.

For all the differences in style that emerged, there was a clear
message from the majority of parents that the mediators' presence had paved the way for a much more creative discussion
than would have been possible without this element of control.
Thus Mr Todd speaks of the mediators' ability to control the
exchanges and, in the same breath, of the way in which this
freed the parents to focus on the children's needs rather than on
their own, 'selfish' preoccupations. Asked about the tone of the
discussion, he replied as follows:

Initially extremely aggressive. They encouraged this to a
degree because they felt that things needed to be said. And
it was very nice being able to say something and have a
mediator there that could prevent fisty cuffs or whatever
else. It was a very controlling influence. The aggression
slowly faded during the interview. There was the realiza-
tion that we had got ourselves into a one to one conflict and
both of us were perhaps . . . had got to the point where we
had stopped considering the children and were really just
out to score points off each other and that became very
apparent very early on and when *both* of us started to
think, my God, this is stupid and what are we doing to the
kids, then the aggression started to fade.

We can gather from this that the mediators' ability to control
the exchanges rests partly on parents' willingness to abandon
mutual recrimination in order to focus on the one interest they
have in common, that is, the welfare of their children. This is
something which most parents attending the bureau have been
unable to manage on their own. In the following chapter we

examine some ways in which the mediators assist parents in making this shift.

Note

1 See, for example, the Report of the Inter-departmental Committee on Conciliation, Part III, para. 3.3.

10

The focus on children

We have already seen that most of our informants considered that authority for decision-making at the bureau remained with them rather than being passed to the mediators. But it was also apparent that the mediators made every effort to divert the parties away from the inter-personal or 'adult to adult' aspects of their quarrel. No matter how angry or embittered they were in relation to one another, they were encouraged to pull in the one direction as far as their children were concerned. So two things were happening at the same time. There was both a 'giving' (of authority) and a 'taking away' (of parents' preoccupation with their own relationship difficulties).

While it would be difficult to argue that the children's interests constitute a wholly independent element in their parents' quarrel, the stress placed on their needs, as opposed to the personal hurt and bitterness of the adults involved, helps to ensure that the discussion is forward-looking, and not simply a vehicle for recrimination. This emphasis on future courses of action, rather than on past events, is characteristic of mediation. Whereas a judge must arrive at his determination on the basis of the facts laid before him, the mediator will look *forward* to the

likely consequences of various alternative courses of action
(Eckhoff, 1969). The corollary of this is that where there exist
major differences between the parties concerning their assessment of the facts, or in terms of underlying values, a mediated
solution is not possible.

Research evidence is now available to support the view of
many legal and 'welfare' practitioners that children's psychological adjustment following marriage breakdown depends, to a
large extent, upon the continuation of a good relationship
between the child and both parents (Wallerstein and Kelly,
1980, p. 316). There is also the view that mediatory intervention
may assist in the development of such relationships (Mitchell,
1985) and a corresponding perception that access disputes, in
particular, can seldom be dealt with adequately through the
formal legal process (Maidment, 1984, p. 42).

The message which the Bromley mediators seek to convey is
that the children, as well as being the focus of the dispute, are
the ones most damaged by it. This shift in attention away from
adult grievances towards an examination of the needs of children is made quite explicitly, echoing the principle which, since
1971, has been enshrined in the legislation governing child-
related issues in the courts, namely, that the welfare of the child
should be 'the first and paramount consideration'.[1] What is
interesting is not only the clarity and persistence of this message but the approval with which it is greeted by most parents.
Mr Parks was a shining example:

> I think what they done really was just sort of pointed out
> faults with the pair of us . . . and made you think, not so
> much of your own petty sort of worries and squabbles,
> more of . . . it's the children, it's the children that are gonna
> suffer. I think it was [mediator]'s words, actually it's the
> children that are suffering, not you two. They sort of got
> you in the frame of mind – you should do what's best for
> the kids – I'd say that still works today actually, with me
> and Laura [wife]. It is basically whatever's good for the kids
> we do. Up until that point it was ourselves that come first.

Mr Todd also accepted the mediators' view that issues
of justice between the adults involved – and the impulse to
recriminate – had to be subordinated to the children's interests.

The eventual agreement was hardly 'fair' from Mr Todd's point of view since he agreed to see one child not at all and the other once a month – much less than he had wanted. Here was a parent whose views exactly mirrored the values upon which the Bromley bureau is based:

> They were trying to get us both to be more reasonable and less hostile and I remember very clearly they explained that it didn't matter a damn about what I thought of my ex-wife or what she thought of me, but what really mattered was the children's welfare, which of course was absolutely right. . . . They certainly defused the situation tremendously. I found them very understanding and very helpful. I didn't necessarily get what I wanted out of it but I think what came out of it was better for the children and that's the whole thing as far as I was concerned – it didn't matter whether my ex-wife was right or I was right. Our differences were *totally* irrelevant in this situation. All that mattered in our case was what was going to cause the children least harm.

Mr Todd's account raises some interesting questions about the nature of mediation in disputes over children. In this instance it would appear that the children's interests were effectively represented by the mediators (always assuming, that is, that they correctly identified those interests). This approach to mediation does not seem to accord with Eckhoff's (1969, p. 171) formulation in which the role of the mediator is defined as 'influencing the parties to come to agreement by appealing to their own interests'. It is possible, however, to see it as an appeal to the parties' common interest in their children's well-being, which would be consistent with the Eckhoff formulation. But the mediators' focus on children is clearly not compatible with a view of mediation as appealing to the parties' interests in any kind of narrow, 'selfish' sense. It is probably more accurate to regard it as an attempt to advance a *third* interest (that of the children).

However, we should be clear that this attempt to focus on children as an independent element in their parents' quarrel does not require the mediators to represent the child's interests in the way that, say, a court welfare officer would be required to do when giving expert advice to the court in order to guide it in its decision-making. Whilst it is not unknown for mediators to present themselves as experts on child development, perhaps referring to research evidence in an attempt to persuade the custodial parent to grant more liberal access, this tactic is employed much more sparingly than in the early days of the bureau. There is now a greater understanding of the problems involved in extrapolating from social research findings to the individual case. There is also a growing recognition that parents' right to make their own decisions should not be regarded as some kind of abstract principle, at odds with child welfare considerations: as far as their own children are concerned, parents may well be the true 'experts', best equipped to determine the arrangements for access and other matters of that kind. Third, some mediators have begun to feel very unhappy about the way in which parents may be subjected to a kind of psychological blackmail, with predictions of harmful consequences for the child if certain courses of action are not followed.

Accordingly, the Bromley mediators are now more inclined to limit themselves to asking the question, 'What is best for the child?' The answer remains a matter for negotiation between parents, who are presumed to be the most competent judges of the issue. This does not mean that mediators have no useful specialist knowledge they can offer, but there has developed greater recognition that this knowledge is at best tentative; that the general principle may not apply in the individual case; and that this expertise should not be paraded in such a way as to browbeat parents.

Both parents are presumed to be concerned for their children's well-being, but of course this 'common interest' perspective does not of itself succeed in eliminating conflict. At the heart of any dispute over custody or access there probably lies some difference of view as to what arrangement would be best for the child. It may be that all the mediators can do is point to the children as the main casualties of the dispute – and therefore the best reason for ending it.

In these circumstances the mediators may be far from 'neutral' in their view of certain proposed solutions, although they will seek to remain 'impartial' *vis-à-vis* the parties.[2] Mr Todd, for example, acknowledged that the mediators did not take sides between him and his wife, but they were nevertheless highly 'partial' as far as the children were concerned: 'They were impartial in the sense they wouldn't take sides but, my God, they were out for the children's welfare and in that sense they weren't impartial. The situation was, what is best for the children? And I think that's the right position to take.'

Several other parents endorsed the mediators' preoccupation with securing an outcome that reflected the children's interests, rather than, necessarily, the wishes of either parent. This was the view of one non-custodial father:

> I think what done it really was that [mediator] put the problem that – Robin [son] was the one who's suffering the most, rather than myself or my wife. And that was what we were there for – it was for Robin and nothing else and we'd got to try and work together and do what we could for him.

Whilst the mediators do their best to persuade parents that they should regard their own differences as of secondary importance (secondary, that is, to the impact of their quarrel on the children), this could be seen – and was seen by some parents – as a means of strengthening the parental coalition rather than an attempt to assume decision-making power. As Ms Harvey explained:

> They pushed it back onto us and made us see that it wasn't fair to be doing what we were doing to Joanne [child]. By not deciding we weren't helping her. And it really made me aware of what I was doing as well and I was really grateful to them for that.

But not all parents felt this. One or two detected the implication that they were not as concerned for the children as were the mediators themselves. Nor, in some cases, did they feel that the children's interests were as easily identified as the mediators implied. The mother quoted below regarded their approach as hectoring and simplistic:

> A lady and a gentleman sat down with myself and Ralph [husband] and asked us what the problem was. And I think Ralph said I would not let him see the children and I said, that's not so. It's because he's so unreliable, that's why he

won't see the children. And the conciliation bureau went
on explaining to me how important it was for children to
see their father and to keep contact and I thought, 'Don't
you bloody tell me that. I know all that'. And that's more or
less a summary.

Even in the above case, certain of the Bromley mediators
might have persuaded this mother that her husband did have
something to offer the children, despite his unreliability, but
unfortunately, in this instance, the force with which the
mediators expressed *their* concern for the child's welfare was
regarded by the mother as a reflection upon the strength of her
own commitment. This extract also serves to remind us that
these disagreements do not arise simply from parents' own hurt
or grief or bitterness (in other words, their more or less 'selfish'
preoccupation with the past marital history). They may
genuinely differ in their assessment of the children's interests.

The view that there is really no dispute in many of these
cases – except that brought about through parents' difficulty in
separating from one another (see, for example, Shepherd,
Howard and Tonkinson, 1984) – is profoundly paternalistic. It
invites the kind of 'therapeutic' approach to divorce disputes
that denies parents the right even to define the nature of their
own quarrel. Nils Christie (1977, p. 4) has argued that both
lawyers and 'treaters' steal conflicts from the parties directly
concerned. Lawyers do this by deciding what is relevant and
then removing the dispute to an arena in which only they have
the competence to perform. Treaters, on the other hand, seek to
convert the image of the case to one of non-conflict – as, one
might say (in the case of family disputes) where parents only
have to be helped in the direction of a generally agreed goal,
namely, the children's psychological health and general well-
being, in order for the problem to be resolved.

Christie was referring mainly to 'conflicts' between victim
and offender and it was in this context that he argued that 'a
non-conflict perspective is a pre-condition for defining crime as
a legitimate target for treatment' (1977, p. 5). But the same
might be said of divorce. According to some parents interviewed
at Bromley, the mediators had conveyed the message that if only
they, the parents, would consider the needs of the child, there

need be no conflict over access. In some instances it appeared that parents went along with this, but in others it was clear that they did not. Or perhaps one parent accepted the reformulation, but the other did not. For example, we find with Mr and Mrs Robb that the wife enthusiastically endorsed the mediators' focus on the children:

> We were told quite clearly . . . that we were there for Meg's [child's] benefit. That was made absolutely clear. We were not there to . . . we hadn't said a word at this point . . . to argue or to quarrel. I suppose they've had other couples there who've become irate for various reasons. I personally had no intention of talking to him other than this re-lationship with Meg's access. But it was made absolutely clear to him, to my husband, that we were there for Meg's benefit. That was, you know, really emphasized. . . . They were not interested really in what had gone before between my husband and I. It was, sort of, let's look ahead, what's happening now with Meg, what can we do to make things better for her? And I felt that immediately and that's why I said earlier on, 'Thank God', because that is the main reason I went to them.

To identify a shared goal – the child's best interests – does not in itself take one very far. There is still the problem of agreeing what those interests are and how they should be pursued – and it is this that is likely to be contentious. Mr Robb, for his part, felt that the discussion at the bureau over the mechanics of access only scratched the surface of the problem. He and his wife did not address what he regarded as the key issues, namely, the difficulties being experienced by their daughter and the reasons why she appeared so reluctant to see him and his new partner:

> My wife and I never had any discussion. I mean, it was all sort of through the counsellors (mediators). We didn't look at each other. The only thing that was discussed was my access to Meg [child] and when it would be. The whole session was one of, well, sort of horse-trading through the conciliators. There was no attempt to move towards any conciliation between my wife and myself.

Where there is a correspondence of view between the mediators and one parent regarding the proper focus for discussion, this may in itself be taken by the other party as evidence of bias. For example, one can imagine in certain circumstances that the mediators' insistence that the parents are there 'in order to help the children' might be viewed by one of them as *a triumph*. In the above case the agreement did not survive. According to Mrs Robb, this was because of her daughter's continuing reluctance to see her father in the midst of divorce proceedings, and second, because of complications arising from Mr Robb's shift rota. A further mediation appointment was offered, but Mr Robb declined to return to the bureau.

It was rather more common for the *custodial* parent to be disenchanted with what, in a few cases, was seen as the mediators' rather naïve expression of concern for the children. One mother echoed Mr Todd's assessment that the mediators had been 'biased in favour of the children', but without the overtones of approval that were present in his statement. She had gathered that the mediators aimed simply to ensure that the children kept in touch with the non-custodial parent:

> Their function is purely to make sure the children see the other party and that's all they're interested in. It's not that they don't care about the situation, but their sole function is to make the children able to see that other person. They are fully biased in the direction they have been trained to go. I felt very, very much that, if you want to put it that way, she was very much on Malcolm's [husband's] side because I had the children. Had he got the children, then perhaps she would've been very much on my side, trying to get me to see them.

The presumption in favour of access

There is no doubt that, unless the circumstances are quite exceptional, the Bromley mediators will seek to promote some form of access agreement. While they will wish to be fair to both sides, the general drift of the discussion will be towards some such arrangement being made.

This presumption in favour of access is consistent with recent trends in judicial decision-making, the leading case being that of

M v. *M* (1973) in which Wrangham J. asserted that access, rather than being a parental right, was 'a basic right in the child'.[3] Recent research studies in this country and in North America endorse that assumption (Wallerstein and Kelly, 1980; Walczak with Burns, 1984; and Mitchell, 1985). These writers acknowledge that not all children want access, and that the *quality* of the experience is important, but they nevertheless convey a very strong message that it is in the child's interests to maintain regular contact with both parents following separation. It is worth noting, however, that these research findings are at odds with the conclusions of Goldstein, Freud and Solnit (1973). Those authors suggest, on the basis of their own clinical experience, that access to the non-custodial parent (usually the father) can be harmful unless there is a positive relationship between the parents. In their view, children have difficulty in profiting from contact with whichever figure is not the key psychological parent (1973, p. 38).

This brings us to the case of Mr and Mrs Lloyd, a couple who had an extremely fraught relationship at the time of their visit to the bureau, with their daughter apparently reluctant to see her father. This was Mrs Lloyd's summing-up of the mediation session:

> I think the only complaint I've got is that . . . obviously, they were impartial, they were prepared to listen to both sides, which is a good point, but I think they obviously took a great deal of store by what my husband said, that I was possibly trying to prevent her seeing him . . . they accepted both versions. You see, they accepted that it *could* be that I was trying to prevent her seeing him. They also accepted that she was very upset and worried and scared of seeing him. They seemed to take both points into consideration, but go ahead and plan the meetings.

Although we do not suggest that some form of access agreement is necessarily the goal of mediation, several custodial parents did feel that the mediators had failed to take seriously the harm being done to the children through the non-custodial parent's erratic or thoughtless behaviour. They resented the implication that it was their influence that lay behind the children's reluctance to spend more time with the other parent.

They felt very frustrated at having to represent their own interests while, at the same time, acting as spokesperson for the child. As Mrs Lloyd put it:

> I felt a little bit as if everybody disbelieved me over her, but I was trying to protect her. . . . I didn't want people to think bad of me. I wanted to do the right thing . . . but on the other hand, no way was I going to force my daughter to do something that was absolutely abhorrent to her.

The underlying question being posed here is that of whether the children can reasonably be said to have a point of view independent of that held by the custodial parent. Many parents insisted that even very young children were capable of arriving at an independent viewpoint. As one mother recalled:

> I had always promised the children – I used to go over and over it and over it – you must do what you want to do. I don't want you to be persuaded by what you think I might think or dad might think or anybody might think, because I wanted their peace of mind. I mean, I didn't want them mucked up at school and for their school work to suffer and all this sort of thing, and if I'm honest, I've heard from the headmaster that children that are under access arrangements did . . . he said you can always tell a child on a Monday morning who's had access with parents because they end up torn. . . . So I thought, well, that wouldn't be the case if this is what the child wants . . . but they continually said they didn't. So under that arrangement I would simply say, you know, they say no. To me, I was their spokesman. I wasn't there to influence what they wanted. They were eight or they were seven or whatever and I felt, as I said before, they should have their choice and I was there to fight for what they wanted.

It is not surprising in these circumstances that some parents argued that the mediators should have arranged a separate interview with the children. In fact, the Bromley mediators do not normally involve children in the negotiations; nor is it usual for the children to be interviewed separately. This aspect of the bureau approach is open to criticism on the grounds that parents and children do not communicate well at this time, so that what

parents say about their children's feelings may differ considerably from what the children themselves say (Wallerstein and
Kelly, 1980; Walczak with Burns, 1984; Mitchell, 1985). But
against this, it can be argued that to interview children would
imply that the mediators were prepared to take on an arbitrating
role. It might also place an unreasonable burden on the child.

The problem, as we see it, is that *one* parent may want the
children to be seen because, at that stage, the children's views
coincide with his or her own. This is no guarantee that the
children would not subsequently change their minds, given
encouragement and opportunity. We therefore regard it as perfectly reasonable that the Bromley mediators see only the
parents. After all, it is the parents' handling of the situation that
is really at issue. This is not of course to deny that children have
a viewpoint of their own – that is something parents understand
only too well. Families make their decisions about these matters in their own way and it is inevitable that the children's
wishes will play a major part. Not infrequently, the whole
thrust of one parent's argument at the bureau was that *the child
should be allowed to decide*. Custodial parents, in particular,
tended very much to see themselves as representing the child's
point of view.

It does not follow from this that the mediators should interview the child, although that is what some parents would have
preferred. Mrs Lloyd was typical in this respect. She felt that
the mediators lacked full understanding of the extent of her
daughter's distress:

I think the one thing that would've really helped, in
addition to what we did have, was for someone in the early
stages, a friendly mum-type lady perhaps, or even a nan-
type lady, to have sat down with Jane [child], possibly in
her own home rather than going to any office or anything
like that, to have sat down and had a general chat with Jane
... on her own ... in a friendly atmosphere ... just
chatting to her generally ... because maybe what happened was dead right, but I'm never going to be sure
because I felt that Jane wasn't really consulted. I put
forward her views as best as I could, being condemned from
his side by, 'You don't want her to see me – you're trying to

stop her seeing me – you're turning her against me.' And
with all due respect, the conciliation bureau had to draw a
line down the middle, but I felt they would've been a lot
more impartial or perhaps been completely guided onto
the right lines with Jane's views ... and they could've
perhaps had a much better view of the right thing to do for
her.

We were in fact told of one occasion when the mediators did
discuss the problem with a (teenage) daughter who was the focus
of an access dispute. The non-custodial mother felt that this
conversation helped her daughter considerably in removing her
fears about access being stopped. She was glad that her daughter's views and difficulties were given independent expression
and were, as a result, accepted by the father, although he still
denied the substance of some of them. Had *she* attempted to act
as a spokesperson for her daughter, she felt sure that her account
would not have been accepted by her former husband.

While the separate interview with the daughter appeared to
work well enough in this instance, it has to be borne in mind
that this was a case where the girl wanted frequent access to her
mother; the difficulty arose from the fact that she wanted the
arrangement to be flexible, so she could see her when *she*
wanted, rather than at times determined by her stepmother.

It seems reasonable to suppose that parents do influence their
children (apart, that is, from explicitly coaching or pressurising
them) but this is not in itself an argument for separate child
interviews. No doubt there are cases where some independent
assessment of the child's feelings would be helpful, perhaps
coupled with an element of counselling or advice-giving (Ross,
1986), but in general it seems to us inappropriate that a mediator
should attempt this. It can only lead to parents' authority being
undermined – something which mediation, in this context, is
intended to prevent.

The mediators' understanding of the history of the dispute

As Chapter 8 notes, some parents argued that a full appreciation
of the children's interests was not possible without the
mediators having some understanding of the recent family
history. For example, one custodial father alleged that there was

already a very disturbed relationship between his daughter and her mother and therefore a reluctance on the girl's part to have any further contact. In this man's eyes, his daughter's reluctance to see her mother – and the reasons for this – were not adequately respected by the mediators. Their focusing on the present and future arrangements and deliberate decision to steer away from an examination of the past meant that in the circumstances of this particular case, insufficient consideration was given to the mother's psychiatric background and unstable way of life:

> You can't really, let's say, make a judgement on one thing without knowing the background, not in my opinion. And they didn't want to know the background. They took someone on their face value, and surely that's not good enough, not when you're dealing with a child's welfare. They took everything that was said, you know, let's say by her, as being gospel.

Here we have another custodial parent who felt that he had the child's interests at heart; it seemed to him that the mediators were committed to one particular standpoint (that access should take place) without understanding all the circumstances of the case. This father concluded that the full evidence could only emerge in court, following examination of the views of the health visitor, doctor and psychiatrist, each of whom knew the family.

Impact of any agreement on the child

Of the 32 individual parents who reported an 'agreement' at the bureau, 21 (66 per cent) said that this had been in the best interests of their children. Our evidence suggests that there were often quite sharp differences between parents in this respect. Thus, of the 8 agreements reached amongst the 12 'couples' whom we interviewed, there were only 2 in which *both* parents said that the agreement had been in the child's best interests. There were a further 2 cases in which one parent thought this and the other was uncertain; whilst in the remaining 4 cases, there was a clear difference of view as to whether the arrangement had helped the child.

A few custodial parents had reluctantly accepted the mediators' advice that perhaps they ought to persuade their children to allow access, presumably in the hope that this would lead to a change of attitude on the child's part. For example, the father who complained that the mediators ignored (or did not bother to find out about) his former wife's psychiatric background had at the time entertained a nagging doubt that perhaps they were right, in which case he should not simply go along with what his daughter was saying. But the outcome was not a happy one:

> I went along with it purely . . . you know, I knew the child didn't want to go but . . . you've got to try, I suppose, haven't you? That was the idea. But unfortunately, it didn't work . . . It certainly didn't help in my particular case, you know. It put my daughter through, let's say, six months to a year of hell.

The case of Mr and Mrs Lloyd provides a further illustration of the possible costs to the child following an agreement at the bureau. Mr Lloyd's initial response had been enthusiastic:

> We reached an agreement. At that time everybody came out thinking, 'yeah, I'm happy with that'. You've got to remember that after not seeing a child for six months, you're quite happy to take whatever you can. I was selfish enough to think that if I left it to the child, she's going to come and see me quite often. I'd do a lot better out of it than having some stipulated times and days per week.

This couple had been referred to the bureau by a judge, following a children's appointment[4] at which Mrs Lloyd had been refused a certificate of 'satisfaction' because access had not been established. This meant that she was unable to obtain a decree absolute. It was in these circumstances that Mrs Lloyd agreed to attend the bureau – and subsequently, gave her reluctant consent to the proposed access arrangement. Of this agreement, she remarked:

> From a selfish angle, yes, I wanted it to happen, but I felt that Jane was really pushed and shoved before she was ready, purely to satisfy the court. I don't say the concilia-

tion bureau pushed and shoved, but they were sort of going along those lines, that access had to be established.

One can see in this case the combined pressures (legal, social and emotional) that may be generated through the presumption in favour of access to which we referred earlier. Whilst an agreement of sorts was reached, the daughter remained in a very nervous, distressed state and Mrs Lloyd now feels that it would have been better had she not been forced to see her father. In the end the pressure placed on her proved counter-productive:

> I think possibly he would have had a better relationship with Jane now, I think, if he hadn't won at that point. Hopefully, she wouldn't be crying on a Sunday morning when he knocks on the door. I sometimes feel she sees him to avoid there being a row between us.

This was a case, in common with many we came across, where the mother was quite capable of seeing the father's point of view and had no desire to prevent him seeing his daughter. The problem lay in the girl's distress at past incidents between her parents, notably the father's violence. As Mrs Lloyd explained:

> She had so many tears and so many upsets and nightmares and everything at that time that I thought it would've been far better – blow the divorce, it didn't make any difference, I wasn't with him anyway – if she could have possibly had even up to a year to settle down and adjust to a new way of life and *then* meet her dad and go out with him. All right, he was frightened he wouldn't be a dad anymore. He was frightened that he would then just be the Father Christmas figure that turned up and took her out. And I can see that point of view too.

Mr Lloyd for his part accepts that his daughter remains unhappy and is uncertain what to do about continuing access. It may be inferred that he also accepts that it was a mistake to put so much pressure on the girl:

> She's having problems. So therefore we're playing it very low key. When it first started my immediate reaction was to go to court and get an order, but I don't think that would

be fair on the daughter. I want her to get over it. I don't quite know how though. That's the trouble.

We've looked at the case of Mr and Mrs Lloyd in some detail because it demonstrates the other side of the coin to the prevailing view that access *ought* to be maintained, except perhaps in the most exceptional circumstances. It has to be remembered that the custodial parent already faces powerful legal and social pressures directing him or her to sustain (and even promote) some form of access arrangement.

Notes

1 The Guardianship of Minors Act 1971, s. 1.
2 We are grateful to John McCrory, Professor and Director of the Vermont Law School Dispute Resolution Project, for some helpful clarification on this point.
3 *M* v. *M* [1973] 2 ALL ER 81.
4 See Chapter 1, note 4.

11

Mediation, gender and power

There is a developing critique of mediation in family disputes which suggests that the present trend towards informal negotiation serves to perpetuate existing power relations within the family (Bottomley, 1984). It is feared that these extra-legal services provide a forum in which the dominant spouse continues to hold sway, unchecked by judicial authority. As a consequence, the real inequality between the parties may be both masked and perpetuated. Compromise between unequals, it is argued, is not necessarily appropriate or just.

It is the woman who is usually thought to be 'at risk' if resort to an adjudicative forum is postponed or effectively denied. In relation to financial or property disputes, or where the man has been violent, it is feared that hard-won gains achieved by women through the courts will be undercut as men resort to these informal modes of dispute resolution. In support of this argument it may be said that the law does indeed provide women with a measure of protection, whilst part of the thinking behind conciliation is the wish to reduce pressure on busy courts.[1] In relation to access, it is again argued that the man, since he is likely to be the non-custodial parent, has more to gain

from the mediation attempt (Wegelin, 1984). In these circumstances, it is he who is in the weaker position (having less
ability to influence children, or to determine the number or
timing of meetings) but, perhaps because it is so difficult to
enforce access orders, the arguments in relation to finance or
violence are seen not to apply. So once again it is the man who
turns to mediation, hoping to achieve through consensus and
moral pressure that which courts have failed to deliver.

To summarize these arguments, it is claimed that no matter
whether the man is in a 'strong' position (finance, property or
physical threat) or a 'weak' one (access), he it is who has most to
gain from mediation, while the woman has most to lose. It has
also been suggested that men and women tend, as a general rule,
to think differently about relationships and moral problems
(Gilligan, 1982). It is feared that this 'different voice' may lead
women, motivated by an ethic of care and responsibility to
others, to disadvantage themselves in untrammelled negotiations with men, motivated as *they* are by an ethic of individual
rights and personal advancement.

There are of course counter-arguments. For one thing, the
problem of power differential does not go away when lawyers
negotiate together on behalf of their clients in the context of
legal proceedings. Where children are involved, women's social
and economic dependence on men will continue to prevail, no
matter what mode of dispute resolution is employed. This
inequality of bargaining power will not lead courts to upset a
private agreement made with full knowledge and advice.[2]

Furthermore, it has to be acknowledged that courts, despite
some recent decisions advancing the interests of women
(Cretney, 1984, p. 253), are male-dominated institutions; their
orientation is certainly not 'feminist'. Rather than giving priority to women, courts, it could be said, give priority to motherhood. Their 'bias', it may be argued, is towards achieving as
close an approximation as possible to the ideal of the nuclear
family in which mother (or mother substitute) stays at home
and father (or father substitute) provides economically (Smart,
1984, p. 213).

Third, it is fair to say that there are many different kinds of
power. These include control of economic resources (including
access to Legal Aid); support from other family members

(including children); physical dominance; and superior negotiating skill. It is important to note that these imbalances need not
be all one way: powerlessness in one area may be compensated
for by (relative) power in another. Nor are these situations
static: the decision to separate may give rise to a radical shift in
the balance of power, say in relation to children.

It has also been suggested that there exists within each
marriage a pattern of *personal* power relations, impenetrable for
the most part to outsiders and possibly unrecognized even by
the couple themselves. Perhaps it is when relationships break
down that people begin to think in terms of power, and it is only
then that these inequalities become manifest (Rose, 1984). No
doubt there are those who will choose *not* to exploit a superior
position, but their spouse may well feel anxious lest they do so.
This anxiety is likely to be compounded because men and
women in these circumstances, feeling vulnerable as they do,
will tend to underestimate their own power and overestimate
that of their spouse.

To date, these matters have been debated in a theoretical
way; they form part of a feminist critique of mediation that
is either unknown to practitioners or not addressed by them.
The few sceptical voices can hardly be heard above the overwhelming professional support for conciliation in each of its
many guises. We believe that our interviews illuminate these
questions and may be of interest to both sides.

At Bromley, as in Bristol (Davis, 1981), we found that it was
usually *one* parent, rather than both together, who had made the
initial approach to the bureau. This appeared to have been the
case in 74 of the 118 cases in the files study (63 per cent). (In most
of the remainder, the couple had either been directed to the
bureau by the court, or had accepted a divorce court welfare
officer's suggestion that they attend.) Within this group of 74
cases, *fathers* (or their solicitors) had made the first approach to
the bureau in 43 (58 per cent) of the cases. Of the 13 non-solicitor
referrals, 10 (77 per cent) came from fathers.

The typical pattern appeared to be for the *non-custodial*
parent to make the initial approach. Amongst those cases in
which the mother exercised day-to-day care, the father made the
first approach in two-thirds, whereas among cases in which the
father had care, these proportions were exactly reversed. This

finding lends weight to the argument that mediation is more attractive to the parent who has least power in determining the current access arrangements. It also suggests why some custodial parents are reluctant to participate.

On the other hand, we found that the women we interviewed at Bromley were actually *more* likely than their husbands to consider that any agreement reached at the bureau had been 'fair'. Of the women who reported an agreement, 86 per cent said this, as against 67 per cent of the men. So this evidence, at least, does not support the view that mediation undermines the position of women.

There were, however, a number of individual accounts that suggested that mediation had indeed served to promote the interests of the non-custodial father in cases where he was seeking more access. This is not altogether surprising given that the mediators' own values support the making of some form of access arrangement. As Chapter 10 shows, some mothers felt that they had to put up with the mediators lecturing them on their obligations to the children, which they believed they understood perfectly well; the only possible value of the proceedings as far as they were concerned was to help the man come to terms with his changed situation:

> The only help that was coming to me was, 'Mrs Webb, it is important that father and children have a relationship with each other', and I felt I knew that more than they could possibly tell me. And I was there mainly to help Ralph [husband] out as to how he wants to handle his children. It might have helped Ralph, I felt as if he wanted the help, not me.

There were other cases in which the woman described the many pressures she was under – health problems, financial and material hardship, coping with ailing elderly relatives, violence – all of which she faced alone. These difficulties rendered quite insignificant the access question that was focused on at the bureau. The woman quoted below expresses very clearly the resentment felt by some mothers in these circumstances:

> I felt that [mediators] didn't understand or appreciate or even want to know about all the problems and all the

difficulties. I mean if I had been better in myself I could've coped with all that, but they couldn't help. They couldn't help me get money. They couldn't help me get shoes for the children. All the things that were, for want of a better word, tormenting me and making my life hell, regardless of the children, had no bearing on those meetings – which was very, very difficult for me, when all they were trying to do was get John [husband] to see the children. I had far more problems to cope with. That to me was a minor problem. All right, to John perhaps it was a major problem, but to me it was very insignificant at the time.

Mrs Dennis made much the same point. She too was pre-occupied with her financial difficulties. What she wanted, above all, was some acknowledgement from her husband that she was having to continue the parenting task alone in difficult and unremitting circumstances. Her efforts were not to be taken for granted:

I don't naïvely expect that I'm going to be maintained or have this meal-ticket for life that everybody's talking about, but on the other hand I have all the commitments with the children and I have the house to run and I do all the things that my husband didn't do. . . . His sort of commitment with regard to the children is geared to their leisure and pleasure and very little . . . OK, he goes to the school and he does this sort of thing, but there's no day-to-day nitty-gritty as I call it. . . . I did find alternative employment which, fortunately, still fits in with what the children do, but if you want me to be blunt, I'm just damned if I'm going to work myself into the ground in order to, you know, relieve my husband of his responsibilities. I really don't think that you can say with any honesty that you want to be a father and want to have a commitment to your children and then opt out of what is basically, you know, the greatest thing of all – which is financial support. He has never messed me about, but on the other hand, it's like getting blood out of a stone. Despite his very much improved situation, nothing is sort of forthcoming, nothing is volunteered, and that really is the nub of my own feeling of very strong resentment.

Mrs Dennis's experience could be seen as lending support to the feminist view that a preoccupation with access serves to undermine the position of the mother and that, despite the rhetoric, the interests of children are in fact secondary, if not incidental, to those of the father. As the Dutch writer, Wegelin (1984, p. 2), puts it:

> Whilst divorced fathers, brandishing emancipation and the biological bond as weapons, crusade for a greater say in the upbringing of their children, public opinion begins to paint the divorced mother as vindictive and abusing her authority . . . the mother is only considered as an obstacle in the way of the father, the child as a pawn in the game.

Wegelin argues that the aim of mediation is normally to achieve access for the father; the mother's co-operation is sought through an appeal to the idea of parents' continuing joint responsibility for their children. This has in practice been collapsed into the notion that fathers should have the right of access. She also points out that these arguments are only employed where parents *dispute* the access arrangements; where the father doesn't bother with access, no one else bothers either.

At the heart of this critique one can again discern Christie's idea (1977) that the full extent of the conflict tends to be played down. The mediators' concentration on what are supposed to be the child's interests enables the parents' clash of interests, and the clash of ideas as to what constitutes the child's welfare, to be safely ignored.

But while the accounts of some parents interviewed at Bromley offer strong support for the feminist view we have outlined, it has to be said that the bulk of our evidence – as may be deduced from the count of answers to the 'pressure' question which is given in Chapter 7 – tends to point the other way. Thus we find that, on the whole, men were more likely than their wives to feel aggrieved at the mediators' stance, often suspecting that their sympathies had lain with the woman. This 'sympathy' did not always imply explicit support for the woman's position, as we shall see, but one message that came through very strongly was that the mediators had been at pains to protect women against the greater emotional force, and in some cases physical threat, that was presented by the husband. In several instances it appeared that bullying had been prevented. Many of the women whom we interviewed acknowledged the support that had been given to them by the mediators. Where such inequality existed, their accounts suggested that the balance was redressed.

Husbands for their part often complained that they had been unfairly discriminated against, or that the woman had been shown special care. Some men implied that they were just as vulnerable, if not more so, than their wives – although this may not have been apparent to the mediators. Mr Bennett was one who felt that the mediators were over-protective of his wife and, in comparison, unsympathetic towards his own position. They failed to appreciate that he too was under stress:

> There was an atmosphere. The gentleman there, he turned round and he said to me like, 'You're a big fella – you're tall, you're big built'. You know, like, no wonder she can't talk, no wonder she's crying. But even so, like, they put me on edge, I mean, I was shaking like a leaf. I don't know what it was. I wasn't distressed by sitting in the room discussing it with other people. If I thought it would have helped or could have helped, I was in favour of it anyway. For whatever good it would've done. I dunno – it was both of them, the man, the lady – they were – I don't know what word you would use for it – very critical of . . . just me. My wife didn't say much at all. They felt quite sorry for her, I think.

Mr Bennett was, as already described, a strongly-built man and the mediators may have been concerned that his more obviously powerful presence would dominate the proceedings. But as far as he was concerned, the mediators' attempt to control the discussion actually made it more difficult for him and his wife to communicate; at least, it hampered his efforts to communicate with her:

> I can't see how they could understand our personal grievances. My wife wasn't really saying what really caused the marriage breakdown and I couldn't say anything because you were only allowed to talk when spoken to. It wasn't like a free-for-all. You could only speak when spoken to. And like, before you knew it, it was over and done with anyway. And like, we never went back.

Mr Bennett would have welcomed a much more robust exchange; in the end, he felt that he had had no 'say' at all. But his wife may have found it difficult to engage with him on this level; what he saw as unnecessary interference and control, she may have experienced as protection and support. As Mr Bennett himself recalled:

> At one point, she [wife] did let off steam, like. She really told me some home truths. Things that I'd wanted her to say but she'd never ever said to me before. But then, like, when I had *my* say, she just broke down and, well, that was that. I mean, like, the gentleman there, he turned round and said to me, like, 'you've got a way with words', or something like that. I'm like a bull in a china shop. I just storm in and then nothing's gained.

The case of Mr and Mrs Selvey offers a rather clearer illustration of how important it may be for the wife that she feel protected by the mediators. As Mrs Selvey describes it, this protection took two forms: first, she was shielded from her husband's verbal bullying; and second, there was the physical protection afforded by the male mediator:

> It was very calm. I could've said anything I wanted to there, which was very important. . . . I suppose it reassured me that in that office I couldn't be bullied, which was very nice. It was comforting to sit down and have somebody civilized, you know what I mean, rather than to be shouted at all the time because of course he couldn't shout in front of somebody else. And that's very nice to be able to go and sit somewhere comfortably because that's what I hadn't been able to do with David [husband] anywhere. Wherever we went it was always screaming and shouting. And [mediator] is so big, you see. It was very nice also to have a man from my point of view . . . that's what I needed because I was being bullied . . . for me it was important that it was a man there.

The mediators often have to grapple with the contrasting verbal styles and methods of argument employed by the marriage partners, although we should not assume that it is always the man who is articulate and belligerent, the woman cowed and retreating. However, our evidence in relation to the Bristol service suggests that some mediators do indeed find it difficult to control the exchanges, this often working to the disadvantage of the wife. Several of the women who had attended BCFCS felt that the discussion had been dominated by the husband, he being more articulate or assertive than they were (Davis, 1988).

It is interesting that BCFCS – an all-female service, with only one mediator working with each couple – seems rather more vulnerable than the Bromley bureau to this accusation of failing to protect the woman from being harangued and bullied by her husband.[3] For all that, we doubt whether the ability to control these exchanges and protect the less outspoken parent is a peculiarly male characteristic. We have seen male mediators at Bromley fail to do this, while some female mediators were anything but inhibited in their challenge to the husband's aggressive behaviour.

In general, it would appear that access disputes present something of a paradox as far as inequality of bargaining power is concerned. Most mediators appear to be at pains to protect the woman against any overt bullying, but in another sense, she may be in the driving seat. One indication of the woman's relatively stronger position is to be found in the fact that of the 18 parents who considered that there had been some change in the balance of the children's loyalties following separation, 15 (83 per cent) thought that they had become more strongly allied with the custodial parent, usually the mother. Where the father appeared to enjoy the mediators' support, one might argue that this was only granted because, in relation to that particular quarrel, it was he who was disadvantaged. It has to be admitted, however, that the mediators' efforts (in Bromley, as elsewhere) are for the most part geared towards remedying the man's disadvantages, rather than those suffered by the hard-pressed single-parent mum on a limited income.

But perhaps the main challenge to the feminist critique of mediation as perpetuating a power imbalance between men and women lies in the mediators' control over the mediation process. If they simply provide a forum in which parents get on with the negotiations without interference, then it might well be argued that in cases where one party threatens to dominate, the mediation attempt will serve to perpetuate this imbalance and give it legitimacy. But some of the Bromley evidence indicates that the mediators did much more than this: they were active; they did challenge; they controlled the ebb and flow of the negotiation; in some cases, the 'weaker' party did indeed feel empowered.

We also have to recognize that the mediator (one, if not both) may develop a greater sympathy for one parent. While not expressed directly, this may nevertheless be significant and, in some circumstances, it could over-ride the mediator's commitment to impartiality. In a few of the Bromley cases it was suggested that a sympathetic understanding had developed between the woman and the male mediator. For example, Mrs Selvey reported that at one point in the interview there was an exchange of glances, following which she believed the mediator took the same view as she did of her husband's behaviour. There is little doubt that from then on she regarded him as being 'on her side'. This is what she had to say when asked if he had understood her position:

> Yes, because then David [husband] came out in his true light for the first time. He started to shout and yell and when he couldn't get his own way he broke down and cried. And that was very typical of the way be behaved, you see. He is like a child still, in this sort of unruly bullying behaviour. And he did that there. And just for a minute . . . [mediator] is very good, but just for a minute, I saw the look in his eyes, you know, and I thought, 'Good, you understand', you know, somebody else has actually seen this because he's very good at covering up. He acts all the time. And I felt more confident then and I came out thinking, 'That's it', you know, 'I don't want to know anymore'.

Much the same sort of thing seems to have happened with Mr and Mrs Robb. The wife in this case spoke very warmly of both mediators and while her response to our question about their impartiality would appear to indicate that in her view they *had* been impartial, she subsequently refers to an 'empathy' with the mediator to whom she refers as 'my counsellor':

> They must be [impartial] because I knew neither of them; they'd never known anything about me. My husband

didn't know them at all. And when they spoke to us together it was obvious that they spoke to us very genuinely and I felt straightaway on the same wavelength. It was impersonal enough that I didn't feel threatened and when I was asked questions on my own, they were not of too personal a nature that I felt that I couldn't answer. I felt I gave them as much as I could and I felt I was getting a lot in return. I liked them both. It appeared to me that my counsellor understood me and although he didn't use any sympathetic words, there was an empathy. Perhaps that was because I wanted there to be, but that was what I felt.

Mrs Robb was not the only parent to have gained the impression that she and her former husband each had their 'own' mediator. This is certainly not intended by the staff of the bureau, but other parents made the same point, although with varying degrees of conviction: 'I got a strong feeling . . . there was a lady and a man . . . I got a strong feeling that the lady took my husband's part and the man took my part. You know, that seemed ridiculous to me at the time.'

Of course, we cannot be certain that these accounts accurately reflect the mediators' stance, although in the case of the Robbs and the Selveys, the accounts of husband and wife were reasonably consistent. In fact, Mr Robb thought that his wife had succeeded in winning over *both* mediators – perhaps not surprising if one accepts his wife's assessment of him as a domineering man who had 'steamrollered' her. It was very gratifying to Mrs Robb that the mediators pointed out the damaging consequences of her husband's behaviour and in effect gave him a reprimand. This explicit recognition of fault was very important to her; she felt that at last someone understood just what she had gone through and how she felt:

I thought the most helpful thing that happened was not only this agreement, but one of the counsellors actually reminded my husband at one point that in fact *he* was the person who left the marriage, who walked out, and yet he appeared to think that he could see Meg [child] when he dictated – I use that strong word, you know, deliberately. He would decide when he would see Meg and I thought this is all wrong. This is all one-sided. This man has totally sort of steamrollered me and now he's doing the same with his relationship with Meg and I'm not going to have that. And one of the counsellors there actually said, 'May I remind you, Mr Robb, *you* are the person who walked out of this marriage?' And I could have kissed him.

It was not surprising in these circumstances that Mr Robb did not feel as kindly disposed towards the mediators as did his wife. When their 'agreement' broke down, he declined to return to the bureau.

It is clear that some mediators, faced with a husband whom they believe is being unreasonable or inconsiderate, are prepared to face him with this. Some men, not surprisingly perhaps, find · this hard to accept. But much depends on how it is done; there were some 'tellings-off' that appeared to be taken with good grace. Mr Rice, for example, expressed himself satisfied with the approach of the mediators, despite the following experience, recounted here by his former partner:

> The person who made the most impression on him was the man, because it was a man and a woman who saw us and we eventually decided on the best possible arrangement. The woman was very weak, I felt. She was around, but she didn't feel like she was really very strong in it. That was the first time. The second time, there was another woman instead of the man. The man had a go at Peter [partner] the first time and the stronger of the women had a real go at him the second time which made me feel a lot better. It was very confirming actually because I was feeling like – I often wondered how much of it was me and how much of it was him. And he really was being so impossible. The original woman was rather weak and didn't really contribute very much, but the other woman was – I mean, she was a real bulldozer.

Similarly, Mrs Dennis, whom we have already heard complain that the real issues (as far as she was concerned) could not be tackled through mediation, was nevertheless delighted that her husband had had a 'dressing down' from the mediator. Indeed, the case of Mr and Mrs Dennis offers a rich vein for anyone seeking to explore the complexities and ambiguities inherent in mediation. This couple attended the bureau three times in all and after the second meeting, an agreement had still not been reached, although it was evident that some progress had been made. Mrs Dennis still felt at that stage that her husband's point of view had dominated the proceedings and she had not succeeded in getting across what she wanted to say; in her own words, she was 'seething'. At the third meeting, therefore, she was determined that there would be no holding back; she was going to tell the mediators and her husband exactly how things stood from her point of view:

> I knew what Michael [husband] was after – he wanted this great big family Christmas with himself and his new lady and his two kids and that was the only reason for all this great big, you know. . . . He wanted it sorted and he wanted me put in the wrong and he wanted it sorted by Christmas Day or whatever. So I was a bit uptight about that anyway. But I walked into this meeting and I thought, well, if the last one's anything to go by, we'll beat around the bush for about three-quarters of an hour, so I just said to [mediator], 'Look, I hope you don't mind but I wrote this down as soon as I got home last time and I just want to say what my thoughts are', so he said, 'OK, shoot'. I went on about this business of duty, commitment . . . all these things came spilling out . . . in the end, it was [mediator] – I know she's got children – she was talking on my behalf.

There are a number of points to note here. First, the mediators ensured that the wife had the opportunity to make the statement that she wanted to make. Second, the things that she wanted to bring home to her husband and the mediators were not about access; on the contrary, she had a whole list of grievances about the way she had been treated – nothing directly to do with her husband's seeing the children. Third, the woman mediator appeared to sympathize with the points made by Mrs Dennis and take up the cudgels on her behalf – in this instance by pointing out to her husband that the children had an independent view of the access arrangements and that this did not necessarily coincide with what he, the father, wanted. Finally, Mrs Dennis had discovered that this mediator had children of her own; she evidently felt that as a result, she was better able to understand and to sympathize with her predicament.

The mediators were seen by both husband and wife as impartial, but it is clear that they gave Mrs Dennis considerable backing. Her husband thought they did this for tactical reasons since it was she who was being asked to make most of the concessions. The quid pro quo for her granting more liberal access was the acknowledgement – initially from the mediators, but then subsequently from her husband – of the problems she faced and the sense of grievance she harboured. Mrs Dennis felt that her husband no longer had any rights in relation to the children; her feelings on this point were acknowledged, but she ended up giving him much of the access that he was seeking (although successfully resisting the demand for 'staying' access).

Mr Dennis had been a little doubtful about the line that the female mediator was pursuing, but he was shrewd enough to realize that she was probably doing this in order to secure an agreement and so he did not object very strongly:

> I felt that perhaps the lady who was doing the conciliation was aligning herself with my wife, not so much to take her side, as it were, but perhaps to help condition my wife a bit to the prospect of making some move. Maybe she felt that she could do it in a way that didn't offend each of us, but I felt slightly aggrieved because I didn't exactly feel the man was on my side, but I felt one of them was on her side. But I realize that tactically it may have been the right thing to do.

This case offers some insight into the nature of the 'support' the mediators may give the mother in these circumstances. It is possible that they may deliberately bolster the self-esteem of the parent who is being asked to 'climb down' in some way. As far as the mediators' support for Mrs Dennis is concerned, therefore, the message is highly equivocal. That such support was offered is undeniable, but the practical outcome of the negotiation favoured her husband. (In another case, that of Mr Todd, we saw the same thing happening, except that in that instance the 'support' was offered to the non-custodial father, he being the one who was asked to make the significant practical concessions.)

All this may sound rather machiavellian, but in fact it is not always clear which parent has gained and which has 'lost' following a mediation session; indeed, such a 'win or lose' approach is expressly rejected by the mediators. Nor should it be assumed that the father is invariably seeking more generous access, while the mother is resisting. The man's plight is not always so pitiful. In fact, a few mothers wished to effect an increase in the father's involvement in the lives of his children. One woman had plied her husband with literature about the possible psychological harm suffered by children following their parents' separation. She had wanted him to see more of his sons. Other mothers had wanted to improve the reliability of access visits, perhaps being concerned about the man's erratic timekeeping. Far from wishing to exclude their former husband, they would have welcomed a greater sharing of responsibility and some respite from the daily grind.

This does not alter the fact that there were many cases in which both sides considered that the wife had been treated more sympathetically by the mediators. However, in these circumstances parents often differed in their interpretation of the mediators' motives. Women, for the most part, attributed their sympathetic treatment to the mediators' acknowledgement of their central position as the custodial parent, or saw it as being due to their greater emotional vulnerability. Fathers, on the other hand, might suggest that the mediators were prejudiced against them, or that they had been overcome by feminine wiles, or third, that their support for the wife had been 'tactical'.

A different light is thrown on this question of the mediators' differential support for men and women through an examination of those cases in which the father exercised care and control, or another group in which access was not the principal issue. What we have seen up to now has to some extent resembled a balancing act between two opposing forces – on the one hand, the mediators' desire to promote access, and on the other, sympathy for the wife and an acknowledgement of the difficulties she faced. But what happens in those cases where the mediators' pro-access orientation does not ally them (practically speaking) with the husband? In the following case, the custodial father concluded that the mediator was totally opposed to his position:

> I think he was totally anti me. He was all for my wife. Which I thought if you're going to reconcile people, you've got to take both sides. And it seemed to me that he didn't. Everything that my wife said was taken as the gospel truth. Everything I said, 'Well, don't you think you could have done this . . . don't you think you could have done that . . .'. It didn't seem to be that *my wife* could've done anything to help. It just seemed all on me and I had to do it. And as I was the one who hadn't left and as I was looking after the children, I thought it was a bit unreasonable.

This man had been hoping for a reconciliation, but the negotiations at the bureau apparently centred on the custody issue, and second, on the related question of which parent should occupy the matrimonial home. At the end of the session, he signed an agreement to vacate:

> I wasn't very happy with it . . . especially having signed a letter saying I was getting out and I would leave my wife with everything. It seemed like they were forcing me to do everything. And I wasn't in a very fit state at the time. I was upset with nervous tension. The shock of it all, sort of, looking after two children all the time. I just signed it to sort of save any more arguments. And to get out of the place as quickly as I could. . . . While we were both in there it seemed to me that the man who was doing it, all he seemed interested in was getting my wife back in here with the children and getting me out. And that's how it struck me. That's all it seemed to be – that my wife was right, I was wrong and I had to do everything to resolve it.

He promptly took his copy of the agreement to a solicitor, who told him that it was worthless: 'I signed a piece of paper stating that I would leave within four weeks and find alternative accommodation, which I took to my solicitor who said, "This has got no legal standing whatsoever, so you stay where you are".'

Having earlier noted the way in which the mediators attempt to smooth the path of a negotiation, paying careful attention to the feelings of the parent who is being asked to give most ground, it is interesting that this man felt that he was granted no such acknowledgement:

> It didn't seem to be any conciliation at all really. Instead of trying to sort of resolve our differences, it seemed like that the man just took my wife's point of view and said to me, 'You're wrong, you've got to go'. And there wasn't really any effort to help me and to help the pair of us get reconciled. I expected it to be more like marriage guidance really. That was the impression I gained from the title of the place, 'Reconciliation Service' (*sic*). I came away in the end literally believing that it had been no help whatsoever. In actual fact it harmed me more than it did anything else. It seemed to me I was the one taking the blame for everything. I was the one totally in the wrong all the time. And I thought I'd been reasonable, myself, in my attitude towards it all.

The following case, again involving a dissatisfied custodial father, was more typical of the bureau's workload in that the dispute centred on the non-custodial parent's access to her son. Perhaps it would be better to call the father in this case 'half-satisfied' since he distinguished between the approaches of the two mediators:

> I basically think that the fellow there couldn't understand the man getting the custody. You know, that type of thing. And it showed . . . with him, you know, the way he was talking to me . . . whereas she done what they were supposed to do. He shouldn't have been concerned about the custody or anything like that. They were there to reconcile between the two parents and the child. And that's what she done in the end. She done it, not him.

In fact, this man became so annoyed at the attitude of the male mediator that he ended up refusing to speak to him. From that point on, all the negotiations were conducted through the woman:

> Now, she was very, very fair, but he was very, very biased towards the wife. I refused to speak to him, I thought he was so biased and I spoke to the woman all the time. He

[male mediator] was getting annoyed but I said, 'I won't speak to you anymore'. I said, 'Do you want to ask me anything?' And this was when the woman interfered. She said, 'Speak through me'. And that's the way it went. It was the woman who sorted it out really. At the end it was solely the woman. I think she told him [male mediator] to be quiet a couple of times. . . . She was very good. She wasn't biased in any way.

In the end, two factors persuaded this father to agree to the access arrangement proposed by the female mediator. The first had to do with her skill in appealing to the one area where he felt vulnerable, namely, his concern for his son. She succeeded in presenting the proposed access as being for the sake of the boy, rather than the mother:

The wife had said that I was refusing to let her see the boy, which wasn't true. The boy didn't want to see her. So after all this screaming and shouting and crying . . . the woman . . . she said, would I help my wife to see her son? So I said, no. So then she put it another way, 'Will you help your son?' So that was it. I had to help the boy. I'll be quite honest, I would've been happier if she'd never seen the boy again, you know. But that was just being selfish.

The other factor leading to an agreement was the pressure this man felt he was under from the court, the case having been referred to the bureau by a judge. A court hearing was scheduled for the following day and the parents had been given the impression that they had to reach agreement before then. Whether it was for this reason we cannot say, but the agreement broke down almost immediately.

Taking parents 'at face value'

A rather different theme, but one that is related to this broad question of men and women's different experience of mediation, arises from some parents' suggestion that the mediators were too ready to accept what their spouse had to say, and also, linked with this, the view of some men that their wives were skilled 'performers' who had succeeded in pulling the wool over the mediators' eyes. (This seems to be the converse of some

women's criticism of their husband's bullying and rigidity;
instead of the domineering husband, we have the devious wife.)
As Mr Rice put it:

> I mean, I must say actually on that first visit, the first time
> we were seen together, Hazel [co-habitee] was absolutely
> transformed. She was a picture of reason – which is a very
> cunning strategy – if you're going to view it as a strategy. I
> could easily have put myself in a position where I was seen
> to be sort of less than reasonable. I mean I don't think it
> was anything as strong as that. But while she sat there say-
> ing nothing, you know, it was difficult to believe . . . that
> she had been the way she was.

Of course, acceptance of a mediation appointment, plus the
influence of the mediators in the course of the discussion, may
herald a *genuine* shift in attitude. Some expectation of change is
inherent in the process. So the fact that parents want to look
good in the eyes of the mediator could be regarded as wholly
positive if it provides the basis for a better future understanding.
Thus the transformation described by Mr Rice, even if viewed
as a 'cunning strategy', could signal something more fundamental – as it appeared to do in his case, both parents being
satisfied with the final outcome and feeling that they had a
greater ability to communicate as a result of their visit to the
bureau.

Mr Rice's suggestion that his former cohabitee may have put
on a 'performance' at the bureau takes us back to Mrs Selvey's
relief when her husband, having initially presented a reasonable
front to the mediator, eventually displayed the overbearing,
manipulative side of his character. This was another woman's
account:

> I remember when I came back [to the joint interview] all I
> got was Roy's [husband's] pain and anguish at your depart-
> ing with the children, and his pain and anguish came over
> so many times, in the end I just wanted to laugh and to say
> to them, 'Well he deserves an Oscar for his performance
> because you're just taken in'. What I said then has come
> true because he doesn't care. He doesn't see his children
> like he should. He doesn't treat them like he should.

But on the whole it was more common to find *men* complaining that the mediators had had the wool pulled over their eyes by those cunning, crafty creatures, their former wives. However, one father distinguished between the mediators in this respect. He thought that his wife had succeeded in manipulating the male mediator (something he alleged she was able to do with most men), but she had *not* been able to do this with the woman:

> I thought that the woman that interviewed me was totally unbiased – I thought that she was brilliant. But I thought the bloke was taken in. My first wife is an attractive, quick-witted woman; she knows exactly how to use men. I'm sure [male mediator] is by no means a fool, but I did go away with the impression that he was biased – only because I was a man – whereas I also went away feeling the woman would have no part of it, that she was totally considering the facts. Perhaps it's because I'd had so much of it over the years and I thought, Oh Christ, here's another one, you know. Whereas the woman, I thought she was sharp, tuned-in, knew exactly what was going on.

This father's comments echo those of certain other men interviewed in Bromley who implied that the male mediator had exhibited a form of 'chivalry'; he may have thought he was protecting the wife against the husband's bullying and verbal aggression, but what came over as far as the husband was concerned was the mediator's sympathetic response to the woman's outward demonstration of distress. These accounts suggest that the female mediators were less easily manipulated (or at least, they were less easily manipulated by other women).

On the other hand, we should bear in mind that these accusations of fabrication and of mediator credulity stem from a partisan source: perhaps the mediators simply preferred not to test these different versions of the truth – which is not in itself a sign of having been taken in. Indeed, it is reasonable to suppose that, on the whole, the use of co-mediators of different sexes will act as a safeguard against the values and perspectives of one parent being allowed to predominate.

Our Bristol interviews enable us to develop this theme. Some of the women who had attended BCFCS complained that their partner was far more articulate than they were – a plausible rogue, even. Their experience was that the one female mediator had been unable to see through the husband's play-acting. So it would appear that the mediators' vulnerability to this 'deviousness' may indeed be related to gender. In Bromley (where there are roughly equal numbers of male and female mediators) rather more men than women complained of their partner's manipulation; whereas with BCFCS (an all-female service) it was overwhelmingly women who alleged that their spouse had duped the mediator – or at least, that he was not pulled up in his play-acting and story-weaving. It may be that mediators are less adept at seeing through 'performances' when these emanate from the parent of the opposite sex to themselves; or at least, they may find it harder to challenge parents of the opposite sex, even if they are not seduced by them.

All this is at odds with the view, held by some of the parents we interviewed in Bristol, that mediators (and indeed judges) will tend to be biased in favour of the spouse who is of the same sex as themselves. Our evidence suggests that for some people it is possible to be understood all too well, so that the inscrutability afforded by sexual difference may lend a little mystery and enchantment, thus enabling the mediator to be taken in.

Notes

1 A substantial part of the *Report of the Inter-departmental Committee on Conciliation* (1983), Lord Chancellor's Department, HMSO, London, is devoted to an examination of this question. See, in particular, paras. 4.1 to 4.26.
2 *Edgar* v. *Edgar* [1980] 1WLR 1410 CA.
3 But see Appendix II on research method, in which it is acknowledged that our sample of BCFCS cases was biased towards that service's 'failures'.

PART 3

The aftermath

12

The ultimate decision-makers

In this penultimate chapter we examine the impact of mediation in the longer term. We have already indicated that in several cases the agreement reached at the bureau was not satisfactory to one or other parent and in some instances it did not survive. We asked all those parents who had reached agreement at the bureau whether or not the arrangement had endured. Replies are given in Table 12.1.

A breakdown rate of over 40 per cent may seem high, but before saying this we really need to know the breakdown rate amongst 'agreements' reached by other means, such as negotiation between solicitors, a welfare enquiry, or a preliminary

Table 12.1 Did the agreement survive?

		(n = 24 cases)
Yes	6	(25%)
In part, with modifications, etc.	2	(8%)
Changed by agreement	5	(21%)
No, broke down	10	(42%)
Other (parent and child emigrated)	1	(4%)

appointment on the court premises. Certainly our research conducted in Bristol suggests that the breakdown rate following an in-court conciliation appointment is higher than that recorded following an agreement reached through the Bromley bureau (Davis and Bader, 1985). One must also recognize that it is somewhat artificial to assess the impact of mediation simply in terms of the durability of an access agreement arrived at in the course of one negotiating session. A better measure would be to try to assess whether, following their visit to the bureau, these parents were better equipped to negotiate together.

In some cases there had been a clear-cut breakdown of the agreement and an absolute cessation of access visits. In a few of these it appeared that the attempt to persuade one parent to accept an arrangement he or she was not really happy with had proved counter-productive. In the following case the mother had apparently agreed to access taking place; however, there are clues in the way the father describes the mediators' handling of the proceedings that suggest his wife had been reluctant to go along with what was being suggested:

> Yes, they were impartial, very impartial. You know, I mean, there was no . . . for her side or my side. It was a frank discussion. I mean, the one that was leading the, I think, the one that was in charge of it . . . he . . . you know, when she wouldn't agree, oh, you know, when she wouldn't answer questions . . . to, you know, things that they put to her . . . when she wouldn't answer them, and I answered my side of it, you know, he talked to her and said, now look, you know . . . you can't get an agreement unless you're willing to say what *you've* got to say. She wouldn't say anything other than what she wanted them to know. And of course, after a while, she started to open up. . . . And I mean, he said, you know, it would be agreeable that if I had the children for the two weeks and then it could be that we could all meet in Croydon and go out shopping somewhere. Or if there was any problem over the children, she and I could meet and discuss it over coffee. Oh yes, she was full of agreement for that. As soon as she walked out of the door she said she didn't want to know about it. She was fully in agreement with it within the confines of the room. Once she got out she changed her mind completely.

A few of the parents we interviewed (mainly men, as it happens) suggested that the bureau should have more power in order to ensure that agreements were observed. One father believed that the mediators should have been able to follow up the agreement in order to see that it was working, and then to give evidence in court if that was necessary. He claimed that his wife had tried to renegotiate the terms of the agreement within days of the appointment. There had followed a series of five court hearings over three years, ultimately resulting in a 'no access' order. Several other fathers (including, as we have seen, Mr Selvey) were disappointed at the mediators' inability to enforce agreements, or to follow them up in any effective way.

It is ironic that this disappointment was echoed by many of those who had experienced the *court's* failure to enforce its own orders. We have already noted that in relation to a particular quarrel, power may be unevenly distributed. In the course of a parallel investigation of custody and access disputes culminating in a court adjudication, it was found that where one spouse was determined to resist the terms of an order, the court often found itself as impotent as any mediator (Davis, 1988). It is clear, therefore, that a successful access arrangement demands the co-operation of both parents. For those who prefer to rely on external authority to settle their differences, this must be an unpalatable message.

The importance of writing agreements down

Given that some agreements break down, we may ask how significant and helpful is the practice generally adopted at the bureau of providing both parents with a written record of any agreement reached. Our evidence suggests that most parents welcome this practice and gain reassurance from it. For example, Ms Harvey commented that she and her former partner needed to refer to this document for quite some time, until eventually they were able to develop a more flexible approach and the written agreement became less important.

Of course, no matter what is committed to paper, an agreement reached at the bureau is not legally binding. Nor is an agreement any more 'solid' for having been written down (although it may, in certain circumstances, have evidential value in subsequent legal proceedings). Nevertheless, there are arguments in favour of a written record. For punctilious parents, it may be reassuring; it gives them something to refer to, even if they cannot force their spouse to abide by it. It may also be useful as a reminder, or as a means of achieving clarification, although in order for that to be achieved the written version must itself be free of ambiguity. Mr Dennis was one parent who attached considerable importance to this document, but he complained that in their eagerness to get something on paper (following three appointments) the mediators had paid insufficient attention to the precise wording:

> We did reach an agreement – I think I ought to qualify that, because those three points that I mentioned earlier were written down and they gave rise to immediate misunderstanding. I mean, within a fortnight. And I think this is why the service was a bit hasty. They were more anxious to have achieved agreement written down than to actually work on the words. I mean, maybe this is because I'm a civil servant and I handle words, but they did lack precision and that's been a problem since. I mean, the timing was such that, you know, I can understand their saying, 'Well, for God's sake, let's get something down, I mean, we're on our way here, we've made a bit of progress'. But it wasn't as precise as it might have been. And I don't mean precision for the sake of it. I mean for both to be clear what we understood by agreeing to this, that and that.

Another argument in favour of written agreements is that the success of all negotiated settlements (including mediated ones) rests on consent and on the moral authority that is gained by each parent being seen to keep their word and act in the children's interests. The fact that parents can demonstrate their adherence to a written agreement may help to sustain their commitment.

Current access arrangements

Of the 39 Bromley cases in which we interviewed one or both parents, 'access' was continuing in approximately two-thirds. (The mean time from mediation appointment to interview was

Table 12.2 Parents' views on current access arrangements

	Custodial mothers (14)		Non-custodial fathers (15)	
Content	9	(64%)	6	(40%)
Not content	5	(36%)	9	(60%)

about eighteen months.) However, even amongst those cases in which access was continuing, there was a 'dissatisfaction rate' (taking each parent separately) of some 50 per cent. Custodial mothers were more likely to express themselves 'content' with the current arrangement than were non-custodial fathers. The figures are given in Table 12.2.

This finding could well reflect the greater control the custodial parent is able to exercise over the access arrangements. But that is not to say that where dissatisfaction was expressed, the custodial parent was necessarily seeking to deny access to his or her former spouse; as we have seen, the nature of the problem was not the same in all cases.

One way of trying to assess the impact of mediation in these cases is to match the outcome of the bureau negotiations, first, against whether or not access was still taking place at the time of our interview; and second, against parents' level of 'contentment' with the current arrangements. Taking first the question of whether *any* access was taking place, we find that amongst the 23 cases in which agreement had been reached at the bureau (excluding one in which the couple were subsequently reconciled) access was continuing in 14 (61 per cent). Of the 14 cases in which there had been *no* agreement (again, excluding one reconciled couple), access was still taking place in 10 (71.5 per cent). The numbers involved are small, but this result is, to say the least, disappointing, particularly as the Bromley mediators tend to set considerable store by the continuance of access. This must say something about the superficiality of a number of bureau 'agreements'.

On the other hand, when we match parents' 'contentment' with the current arrangements against the outcome of the mediation session, a much more positive picture emerges. (This question was only asked if access was continuing; the calculations that follow exclude all cases in which there was no current access.) We found that where agreement had been reached at the appointment and access was continuing (n = 19 individuals), 12 of this group (63 per cent) expressed themselves content with the arrangements. By contrast, where *no* agreement had been reached at the appointment but access was continuing (n = 13 individuals), only 4 parents (31 per cent) expressed themselves 'content' with the current arrangements.

Whilst we have too few cases for these figures to be reliable, they do suggest that agreement at the bureau is associated with a higher level of parental satisfaction with subsequent arrangements, always supposing that access continues. There is a possibility, however, that parents who reach agreement at the bureau may in general be less bitterly opposed, or more flexible than those who do not; in other words, their relative 'contentment' may be due to their greater capacity to negotiate together. The agreement at the bureau may have been a reflection, rather than a cause of this. Even if this were the case, the bureau still provided the forum in which this potential for agreement could be realized. We cannot assume that there would have been a similar outcome had mediation not been available.

Impact of mediation on the relationship between the parents

One of the most clear-cut findings to emerge from this study is that the Bromley bureau serves mainly to secure practical, workable access arrangements, rather than to effect some kind of transformation in parents' relationship with one another. Although 32 individual parents reported an 'agreement' at the bureau, fewer than half of these believed that their relationship with their spouse had been significantly altered as a result. Indeed, 26 of those interviewed were still anticipating a court hearing on some aspect of their divorce – usually finance. On the other hand, it is reassuring that of the 19 parents who reported a failure to reach agreement at the bureau, there was only one who said that her relationship with her former spouse had deteriorated as a result of this failed negotiation. Mr Todd was one parent who made it clear that there was still no love lost between him and his former wife, but the fact that a workable access arrangement had at last been agreed meant that he was no longer preoccupied with his feelings of resentment towards her:

> Although the bitterness never entirely goes and one always feels a bit resentful about what one's ex-partner's done, the beauty of the whole thing is that now I can sit back and say, what they managed to achieve for us was the best that could be done in the circumstances for the children's sake and there is absolutely no point in worrying about the fact that I consider my ex-wife was an absolute bitch over some things. It's irrelevant. It's gone. They defused it completely and I can now live a normal life rather than spending all my time going round with high blood pressure and, 'God, I'm going to get her' – which was the state I'd got into. It's no good to anybody. It's no good to yourself, it's no good to the people around you. Your work performance goes down. Your own personal relationships get very strained, although my [second] wife in fact was extremely supportive. But she must have gone through hell for a long time. So yeah, they did a marvellous job from that point of view.

Mr Rice was another non-custodial father who thought that the emphasis placed by the mediators on his role in relation to the child had helped bring about a change of attitude on the mother's part:

> The sort of thing that was said on the first joint interview was that it is for Joanne's [child's] good; you can't pretend I don't exist and I was sort of being, I suppose, fairly aggressive about it; and she of course said, 'Well, yes, of course, what's the problem?' And it looked like I was being the great aggressor, but there was actually a remarkable turnaround in that 'Yes, of course'.

In this case, as it happens, the negotiations at the bureau led to an improvement in all aspects of this couple's relationship, as Ms Harvey made clear:

> I was sort of uncertain about what either of them were going to achieve actually, or were going to help us achieve. I didn't have a lot of confidence in either of them to start

with, but I did feel a lot of respect for them by the end. And I certainly have a lot of respect for them now because I think what they helped us to do was really helpful and very resolving.

But the case of Mr Rice and Ms Harvey was unusual in the degree to which they considered that the mediation sessions (two in their case) had led to an improvement in their own relationship. Several parents made the point that one should not ask too much of mediation. They thought it unreasonable to expect the restoration of a harmonious relationship. As one woman explained:

> You see, I think maybe people expect too much of these things. In a situation where you've got a marriage that's broken up like this, you've got two people who are claiming things against each other and any impartial visitor hasn't got a clue who is telling the truth and who isn't. And in the middle of it, you've got these poor kids being pulled from pillar to post. A conciliation bureau can't possibly be capable of making everything in the garden lovely again, because life just isn't like that and they've got to accept that – if they're going to always try to make everything lovely, well they're just not going to succeed and it's going to be a sort of ridiculous situation, and they're going to feel they've failed. In fact they haven't failed . . . if only an unbiased, trained person can be there as guidance . . . they've done a very valuable job. I think they tend to feel that they've failed if they haven't made everyone all happy and loving again. But they haven't.

The mother quoted here seems to us to have got it about right – or at least, her views concerning the appropriately modest goals of mediation coincide with many parents' experience of the bureau. It was quite common, following an agreement reached through mediation, for there still to be an element of strain between the parents, this being played down for the sake of the children. As another parent explained:

> Her dad and I, oh we have our ups and downs still, we have our little . . . I feel sometimes I could say something . . . but

I think no, we've got to keep the peace for the children. I never ever pull her dad down and hope he hasn't . . . we've been able to communicate more, which I think has helped Lynne [daughter] tremendously.

From this non-custodial mother's point of view, the benefits her daughter gained from the more relaxed access arrangement made it more than worthwhile to swallow any little resentments that she (the mother) still felt towards her former husband:

It did affect her school work, with the problems she was having – not being able to get on with her step-mum and all the other problems. But since going to the conciliation bureau we've had the most marvellous rapport going. Really, because she's been able to voice what *she* feels and she can talk to me a little bit more now and of course her dad – she's always coming home and saying, 'Daddy's done this' – and she's pleased with herself. And it really has helped her education tremendously.

The ultimate decision-makers

In the course of our research we were given a great deal of positive 'feedback' from parents concerning the work of the Bromley bureau. Nevertheless, it would be wrong to give the impression that the mediation session (or sessions) at the bureau proved to be the over-riding influence upon these families' future access arrangements. It is important to understand that in the end, parents and children work these things out for themselves. Negotiation continues *after* the meeting at the bureau. This does not mean that the mediation attempt was insignificant – it may well have played a very important part in the process whereby parents (some of them) managed to come to terms with one another.

Perhaps the most dramatic illustration of this is provided by the two couples who subsequently reconciled. There was no clue at the time in either case that this would be the eventual outcome. One couple were unmarried and the woman summed up their dispute as 'a petty little thing' that 'snowballed'. She said of her partner, 'I think he didn't realize what he was letting himself in for really'. Once all the third parties (solicitors, judge and mediators) left them alone, they sorted out their own affairs.

The other reconciliation occurred in the case where the man had signed a written agreement promising to vacate the matrimonial home. When he subsequently went back on this undertaking, his wife tried to remove the children from his care, whereupon he embarked on wardship proceedings. Within a day of the papers being served on her, she resigned her job and returned home.

The case of Mr and Mrs Bennett is not dissimilar in that the really dramatic improvement in their relationship occurred *after* their visit to the bureau. They now have friendly, frequent contact. Mr Bennett would like to remarry, but Mrs Bennett says that she is happier as she is. She is jealous of her newly-attained independence and privacy, although she welcomes the contact with her former husband.

Of course, in this as in several other bureau cases, the mediators' intervention (specifically, their advice to avoid raising any contentious matters in the course of access handovers) may have contributed to the parents' better understanding. But in some instances it was difficult to discern any direct contribution from the mediators. For example, one couple had had a violent disagreement at the bureau, whereupon the wife had walked out. The husband was subsequently granted an order for defined access by the court and there was also a financial hearing, out of which the mother did very well. From her resulting position of strength she made sympathetic overtures to her husband and went out of her way to ease the tension between them, including allowing more frequent access visits. Her conciliatory attitude led to an improvement in their relationship and the access arrangements are now much more flexible.

Another couple reached an agreement of sorts at the bureau, but the husband decided that this was very unfair to him and within months took court proceedings in order to get more access. The defined access order made by the court was identical to the agreement worked out at the bureau, but since then this couple have themselves worked out an arrangement that suits them both and is flexible. The children organize much of the contact with their father and he has a good relationship with them, although he would like even more access. The parents communicate easily, although they are not friendly. As the mother explained, 'We've sorted things out more now than what we did in court or through the conciliation bureau, not that we've sat down and talked, but as the time's gone on I've let him have the children more because sometimes it suits me and obviously sometimes it suits him.'

The fact that some parents do in the end appear to work things out for themselves is not, of course, incompatible with the aims of mediation. The mediators' objective, after all, is to help the parties achieve a greater capacity to negotiate together. It is against this yardstick, rather than the number of agreements reached in one or two negotiating sessions, that mediation should be judged.

13

Conclusion

There is now a growing literature devoted to the organization and conduct of divorce mediation, most of it written by practitioners. There is also a developing academic critique, much of it with a limited empirical content. This book does not fall into either camp; instead, we have attempted an analysis that is rooted in the practice of one mediation agency. The consumer perspective was a vital ingredient in this, although we should stress that, as with any other empirical research method, consumer accounts do not provide 'the answer': they are simply one route, albeit a very illuminating one, by which the researcher may hope to provide a coherent and plausible account of what goes on.

In reflecting on the key messages arising from our research, one can see that these fall into the two broad areas of

1 service organization; and
2 practice method and skill.

That is not to imply, of course, that there is not a close relationship between these two realms: the organizational framework within which a service operates, influencing as it

does such matters as the degree of authority vested in the practitioner, will have a decisive influence upon work methods. This
is especially true of mediation, where questions of authority are
so central and so delicate. Nevertheless, we believe it reasonable in this final chapter, first, to review the organizational implications of our research, and second, to draw attention to some
lessons for mediation practice.

Organization

We have noted that the divorce court welfare service, attracted
as it is to 'conciliation', wishes to apply this idea, with its
associations of reasonableness, compromise and the pursuit of
common interests, to its statutory responsibilities. Accordingly, welfare officers are seeking to integrate elements of conciliation into their core activity, this being the investigation of
children's circumstances on behalf of the court. However one
describes the practice hybrid which then results, it is inescapable
that welfare officers operate within a judicial, and so, ultimately, a coercive framework. The same may be said of the
attempt to offer conciliation on court premises, whether this
be in the context of a contested custody or access application,
or of a s.41 children's appointment, the latter being the child
welfare checking mechanism routinely employed by courts.

At Bromley we have studied the attempt made by one statutory welfare agency to provide a non-coercive mediation service
for those parents who wish to avail themselves of it. It can be
seen that the Bromley bureau is itself a hybrid: first, because it
offers a voluntary mediation scheme while being closely linked,
in terms of administration and personnel, with the statutory
court welfare service; and second, in that it accepts referrals
from the court and from welfare officers, thereby contributing in
some instances to the settlement of legal issues. Even so, the
bureau operates a form of conciliation that has much more in
common with that of independent services, such as BCFCS in
Bristol, than with the model being developed in some areas as an
integral part of court welfare practice (Shepherd, Howard and
Tonkinson, 1984).

To conciliation-minded welfare officers, the bureau's attempt
to separate mediation from court process may appear tortuous

and pedantic. This is because welfare officers are concerned, laudably in our view, to improve their practice *as officers of the court*; they do not regard it as part of their business to provide a non-statutory mediation service in addition to and separate from these other responsibilities. However, our research demonstrates that some parents do indeed welcome the opportunity presented by the Bromley bureau to opt in to a form of conciliation that is presented as an entirely separate option, rather than as a lubricant to third-party decision making. Provision of this separate service in South-East London reflects a sensitivity to the issue of authority and a recognition that, for some parents, the ability to resolve potentially explosive issues *without* submitting themselves to professional experts is something to be valued in its own right. Fred Gibbons and his colleagues deserve to be congratulated on having identified this aspiration and given it expression, even if the fact of their operating under the court welfare umbrella gives rise to awkward presentational problems and some genuine difficulties of organization.

Given this relatively heartening message, it is unfortunate that the prevailing view appears to be that a service which is truly independent of the courts will attract few customers. A low caseload makes for an uncertain future, so the genuine commitment of the Bromley bureau to offering a non-coercive approach to divorce disputes could be undermined by these pressures to provide a court-related service.

This might lead one to conclude that mediation services belong most naturally in the independent sector, on the basis that pressure to provide a service for the courts can be resisted more easily there. In fact, this may not be the case, given the shortage of funds suffered by most independent schemes. Many have bent over backwards to establish links with local courts – the closer the better. Given the pressing need to achieve a secure financial base, this is hardly surprising, but it does compromise any claim these schemes may make to being 'independent'. It is possible that the divorce court welfare service is better placed to resist these pressures, although that assumes, first, that welfare officers will think it worthwhile to provide such a service; and second, that probation committees will endorse the inevitable diversion of resources which this would entail.

Outcome measures

Before reflecting on the main conclusions one may draw from our study of mediation process, it is as well to acknowledge that we attach limited importance to the question of the Bromley mediators' 'success-rate', measured in terms of agreements reached on the day. One of the reasons for conducting consumer interviews was to go beyond the mediators' own assessments. Our interviews revealed that in some instances the appointment was quite insignificant, whatever the recorded outcome, whereas for other couples an appointment that gave rise to an apparently equivocal outcome contributed to a lasting improvement in relations.

It was also interesting to observe that where more than one appointment was held, the outcome at the first meeting tended to be confirmed on any subsequent visit to the bureau. Even the mediators' tentative and uncertain verdict 'some progress' was usually replicated on a second occasion. This is perhaps disappointing, but it is likely that family circumstances among this group of cases were such that 'some progress' was all that could reasonably be expected. As Chapter 12 indicates, we believe that the bureau's work – indeed, any attempt at mediation in family disputes – should in general be assessed in terms of the parties' improved negotiating capacity, rather than through the use of more absolute (and final) concepts such as 'agreement' or 'failure to agree'.

A second reason for our wishing to undertake consumer interviews was that we wanted to place the one or two negotiating sessions at the bureau in the context of the dispute as a whole. One of the strongest messages to emerge from our interviews was that these couples regarded their disputes as arising from unique personal circumstances. They felt that these special elements had to be taken into account – something the legal process, in their experience, had failed to do. An important characteristic of mediation is its 'procedural flexibility' (McCrory, 1981, p. 56). This enables all the ramifications of the dispute to be taken into account, including each person's emotional vulnerability and the ethical stance they choose to adopt. These elements contribute very significantly to each party's view of events and it is appropriate that they be allowed expression in the give and take of negotiation.

This brings us back to our earlier point, that in measuring the 'success' of the mediation effort it is necessary to take a long-term view. The resolution of access disputes requires the active co-operation of both parents over a long period. This is not encouraged by the competitive strategies that are required in order to mount a successful legal case. Our interviews revealed that, in some cases at least, mediation greatly enhanced the parties' capacity to negotiate together; without this assistance, their potential for co-operation would not have been realized.

Mediation practice

Mediation practice is contingent upon the organizational framework within which a service is offered. It was in recognition of this fact that, in our introductory chapter, we posed the question: does mediation, via a service that is closely linked to divorce court welfare and that calls upon some of the same personnel, succeed in giving back authority for decision-making to parents? On the whole, the evidence of our interviews supports the stated position of the bureau – which is that responsibility for decisions does indeed rest with the parties.

The corollary of this, one might have thought, is that the mediators cannot compensate for any imbalance of power that may be suffered by one parent. But that is only partly true. The mediators do not determine the outcome of the negotiation, but the importance of their focusing the discussion and ensuring protection, in that setting, for the more vulnerable spouse can hardly be over-stated. This form of 'authority' is perfectly compatible with a mediating role and it was manifested, although not altogether consistently, by the staff of the bureau.

Successful mediation rests upon adherence to certain key values, notably those of mutual respect and equality of exchange. The tone is set by the meditors themselves, in the way in which they treat the parties and each other – that is, ideally, with dignity and respect. Lacking the procedural safeguards of due process, mediation relies upon the parties' adherence to these standards. The Bromley mediators have developed certain structures by which they hope to emphasize these (the separate initial interview; the 'feedback' to both parents jointly; the use of co-mediators, one of either sex) but in the end it is up to parents to decide whether they can go along with the message of collaboration and 'reasonableness' that is being conveyed. Their decision to attend the bureau in the first place, assuming they were not operating under a misunderstanding, suggests a willingness to do so. At the same time, it should not be assumed that mediation is only appropriate for those couples who are able to conduct a relatively harmonious divorce, or whose disagreements in relation to children are based on a misunderstanding. Our interviews suggest that considerable progress was made even in cases where the parties had come to regard one another with animosity and distrust.

This throws new light on the vexed question of the 'demand' for mediation. It seems to us that this is a reflection, not simply of the level of publicity these services attract, but of two key components of the mediation process:

1 the mediators' use of authority and management of power differentials; and
2 the mediators' values and assumptions in relation to the substantive issues (especially access).

Mediation has to appeal to both parties and it will only do so to the extent that it has the potential to benefit both, rather than to provide a vehicle through which one parent can bring pressure to bear on the other.

It is for this reason that the evidence in relation to gender provides some of the more challenging insights to emerge from our study. To some extent the presumption in favour of access leads the mediators to be sympathetic to the case advanced by the non-custodial parent (usually the man). On the other hand, the growing sophistication of the Bromley mediators was apparent in their willingness to consider a *range* of issues so that many negotiations encompassed a variety of post-separation difficulties and grievances. This is an important point: it is unreasonable, in our view, to criticize family mediation because of its failure to remedy structural inequalities in our society, but what one can ask is that the parties' perceptions of their social and material circumstances not be ignored by the mediators. In general it appeared that the bureau staff were quite prepared for these matters to be included in the discussion. We heard, for example, of several custodial mothers who had demanded explicit acknowledgement from their former spouse of the harshness of their predicament as a lone parent bearing the entire burden of child care, all on limited resources of energy and finance. Similarly, non-custodial fathers sought recognition that they still had an important role to play in their children's lives. They felt acutely vulnerable in circumstances where step-fathers had daily contact with their children while they themselves were restricted to perhaps fortnightly visits. They wanted some acknowledgement of their vulnerability, and of the emotional costs involved.

The mediators' carefully fostered even-handedness was also reflected in the way in which they jealously guarded each party's right to free expression. This concern for procedural fairness is a vital feature and one that needs to be sustained if mediation is to develop its appeal. Fairness in relation to outcome is in some ways less important since no conclusion reached at the bureau is legally binding and we generally found that parents chose not to stick to the fine print of an agreement in any event.

The fairness of the mediation process may therefore be said to rest upon two aspects: first, protection and even-handedness in the management of the negotiation; and second, even-handedness in respect of the mediators' concern for the *objectives* of each parent. In both respects the Bromley bureau has developed a characteristic mode of operation and one that is welcomed by the majority of its customers.

In relation to outcome, the focus on children's interests – which, as we have seen, is made quite explicit by the mediators – was notably effective in mobilizing the most powerful of all motivations for collaborative effort. However, as Chapter 10 notes, it was not the commitment to advance the welfare of children that caused difficulty, but rather the question of how this was to be achieved. Thus, whilst the mediators' stress on the children's interests was generally welcomed by parents and proved remarkably liberating in a few instances, there were several other cases in which the identification of those interests proved contentious. There was often little the mediators could do about this, except perhaps encourage parents to adopt *the child's* perspective on the issue when this appeared to be being neglected. Needless to say, it is essential in these circumstances that the mediators do not regard a failure to reach agreement, or a preference for court adjudication, as an indication that parents do not have the best interests of their children at heart.

In general it appeared that the mediators were on surer ground when seeking to overcome failures of communication between parents, and when pointing to the children's suffering as the best reason for ending the conflict, than they were when attempting to promote their own solutions. It would appear that, in practice, the Bromley mediators are not always as self-effacing as the 'facilitator' definition of their role might suggest. It should be emphasized, however, that the pressure to reach a specific agreement, whilst real enough, was far less than 'at the door of the court', or in the context of a preliminary appointment on court premises, when lawyers' preoccupation with securing legal settlement can leave parents powerless and uncomprehending. Discussion at the bureau was much more likely to facilitiate communication and so to leave parents in a position to manage *future* negotiations.

This is an appropriate point on which to end since it returns us to one of our main themes, namely, the importance of sustaining mediation as a service separate from and independent of the court – the kind of service, in other words, of which it may genuinely be said that parents have *nothing to lose* if they choose to avail themselves of it. Our survey of customers of the Bromley bureau has demonstrated that, for some couples, there may also be a great deal to gain.

Appendix I

Background information about the couples within our interview sample

Employment/social class

Between a quarter and a third of the couples in our interview sample were drawn from the Registrar General's social class II (teachers, nurses, policemen, etc.). This is a higher proportion than amongst the divorcing population as a whole. Also, 22 of the 24 women whom we interviewed in Bromley told us that they had worked during their marriage (either full or part time). Of these, 14 (58 per cent) had worked full time. This is a considerably higher proportion than amongst the divorcing (or indeed the married) population as a whole. At the time of interview, 9 of the women (37.5 per cent) were working full time and a further 8 (33 per cent) were working part time.

Unless there has been a significant distortion arising from our refusal rate, these figures suggest that the bureau's clientele tend towards the 'middle class', both in relation to the man's category of employment and to the greater likelihood of the woman being in work following separation.[1]

Care arrangements

Of the 39 cases in our interview sample, there were 2 in which the parties had become reconciled. Of the remaining 37 cases, all of which involved dependent children, the mother exercised care and control in 31 (84 per cent), while the father did so in the remaining 6 (16 per cent).

Notes

1 For comparative information, see Davis, G., Macleod, A. and Murch, M. (1983) Divorce: Who Supports the Family?, *Family Law*, No. 7.

Appendix II

A note on method

As Chapter 4 notes, our files sample of 118 cases comprised all those couples who had experienced a joint mediation appointment at the bureau in the period from its inception in July 1979 to the end of March 1982. The interview sample was drawn from cases referred to the bureau between July 1981 and March 1982 – which means that they had also featured in the files study. Our 51 interviews were drawn from an initial sampling frame of 52 cases, these being all those couples, actually seen together, who had been referred to the bureau in the above nine-month period. This occurred as follows:

Initial sampling frame	104 individuals
Not allocated (either because of distance,[1] or address not known, or believed to be in poor health)	17 individuals
Allocated but not traced (moved and no forwarding address)	7 individuals

Of the remaining 80 people with whom we made contact, our interview 'success rate' was as follows:

	(n = 80)	
Interviewed	51	(64%)
No reply to letters[2]	12	(15%)
Declined to be interviewed	17	(21%)

We matched out interview 'success rate' against the outcome of the mediation session(s) recorded at the bureau. The result was as follows:

	Agreement	No agreement
Cases in which we interviewed *both* parents	67%	33%
Cases in which we interviewed *one* parent only	59%	41%
Cases in which we interviewed *neither* parent	73%	27%

In short, there was no discernible pattern. So our sample was not biased towards demonstrably successful outcomes, although it has to be borne in mind that recorded agreement is a very rough and ready measure in any event. We still cannot be *certain* that our sample was not weighted towards parents who held a positive view of the bureau.

BCFCS

Occasionally in this book we have made reference to some interviews we conducted with 'consumers' of the Bristol Courts Family Conciliation Service. But it has to be emphasized that the 61 former clients of BCFCS cannot be regarded as representative of that service's clientele. Our sample was in fact heavily weighted towards the service's 'failures'. This was due simply to the fact that we obtained these cases from the lists for trial at Bristol County Court. BCFCS is primarily (although not exclusively) a *pre-litigation* service. The cases we came across therefore were those in which:

1 no agreement could be reached through mediation; or
2 the agreement had subsequently broken down.

The only exceptions to this general rule were, first, any cases referred to BCFCS *after* court proceedings commenced; and second, any cases in which the issue before the court was not the same one as had been 'conciliated'.

Notes

1 More than twenty miles from Bromley, approximately.
2 This group, who all lived too far away for us to call on the off-chance, can for the most part be taken to have declined an interview, although we cannot be certain that they had all received our letter.

Bibliography

Abel, R. L. (1982) The contradictions of informal justice, in R. L. Abel (ed.), *The Politics of Informal Justice*, Vol. 1, Academic Press, New York.

Auerbach, J. S. (1983) *Justice Without Law?*, Oxford University Press.

Bernard, J. (1982) *The Future of Marriage*, Yale University Press, New Haven.

Bottomley, A. (1984) Resolving family disputes: a critical view, in M. D. A. Freeman (ed.), *State, Law and the Family*, Tavistock, London.

Bottomley, A. (1985) What is happening to family law? A feminist critique of conciliation, in J. Brophy and C. Smart (eds.), *Women in Law*, Routledge & Kegan Paul, London.

Brown, A. (1977) Worker-style in social work, *Social Work Today*, Vol. 8, no. 29.

Christie, N. (1977) Conflicts as property, *British Journal of Criminology*, Vol. 17, no. 1.

Coogler, O. J. (1978) *Structured Mediation in Divorce Settlement*, Lexington Books, D. C. Heath and Company, Mass.

Cretney, S. (1984) *Principles of Family Law*, Sweet & Maxwell, London.

Davis, G. (1981) Report of a research to monitor the work of the Bristol Courts Family Conciliation Service in its first year of operation, *30th Legal Aid Annual Reports, 1979–80, app. D*, HMSO, London.

Davis, G. (1983) Conciliation and the professions, *Family Law*, no. 1.

Davis, G. (1983a) Mediation in divorce: a theoretical perspective, *Journal of Social Welfare Law*, May.

Davis, G. (1988) *Partisans and Mediators*, Oxford University Press, Oxford.

Davis, G. and Bader, K. (1985) In-court mediation: the consumer view, parts I and II, *Family Law*, Vol. 15, March and April.

Davis, G., Macleod, A. and Murch, M. (1982) Special procedure in divorce and the solicitor's role, *Family Law*, Vol. 12, no. 2.

Dingwall, R. (1986) Some observations on divorce mediation in Britain and the United States, *Mediation Quarterly*, no. 11.

Eckhoff, T. (1969) The mediator and the judge, in V. Aubert (ed.), *Sociology of Law*, Penguin, Harmondsworth.

Eekelaar, J., Clive, E., Clarke, K. and Raikes, S. (1977) *Custody after Divorce*, Centre for Socio-legal Studies, Oxford. SSRC publication.

Felstiner, W. and Williams, L. (1985) Community mediation in Dorchester, Massachusetts, in S. B. Goldberg, E. D. Green and F. E. A. Sander (eds), *Dispute Resolution*, Little, Brown & Co., Boston, Mass.

Freeman, M. D. A. (1981) Towards a more humane system of divorce, *Justice of the Peace*, 21 March.

Freeman, M. D. A. (1984) Questioning the Delegalization Movement in Family Law: Do We Really Want a Family Court? in J. M. Eekelaar and S. N. Katz (eds), *The Resolution of Family Conflict*, Butterworths, Toronto.

Fuller, L. L. (1971) Mediation – its forms and functions, *Southern California Law Review*, 44, pp. 305–39.

Gilligan, C. (1982) *In a Different Voice*, Harvard University Press, Cambridge, Mass.

Goldstein, J., Freud, A. and Solnit, A. J. (1973) *Beyond the Best Interests of the Child*, Free Press, New York.

Gulliver, P. H. (1979) *Disputes and Negotiations: a Cross-cultural Perspective*, Academic Press, New York.

Irving, H. H. and Benjamin, M. (1984) A Study of conciliation counselling in the Family Court of Toronto: implications for socio-legal practice, in J. M. Eekelaar and S. N. Katz (eds), *The Resolution of Family Conflict*, Butterworths, Toronto.

James, A. L. and Wilson, K. (1986) *Couples, Conflict and Change: Social Work with Marital Relationships*, Tavistock, London.

Kressel, K. (1985) *The Process of Divorce*, Basic Books, New York.

Maidment, S. (1984) *Child Custody and Divorce*, Croom Helm, Beckenham.

McCrory, J. P. (1981) Environmental mediation – another piece for the puzzle, *Vermont Law Review*, 6, no. 1.

McDermott, F. E. (1975) Against the persuasive definition of self-determination, in F. E. McDermott (ed.), *Self-Determination in Social Work*, Routledge & Kegan Paul, London.

Minuchin, S. (1974) *Families and Family Therapy*, Tavistock, London.

Mitchell, A. (1985) *Children in the Middle*, Tavistock, London.

Mnookin, R. H. and Kornhauser, L. (1979) Bargaining in the shadow of the law: the case of divorce, *Yale Law Journal*, Vol. 88, p. 950

Murch, M. (1980) *Justice and Welfare in Divorce*, Sweet & Maxwell, London.

Parkinson, L. (1983) Conciliation: pros and cons (I), *Family Law*, Vol. 13, no. 1.

Parkinson, L. (1986) *Conciliation in Separation and Divorce*, Croom Helm, Beckenham.

Pearson, J. and Thoennes, N. (1984) Custody mediation in Denver: short and longer term effects, in J. H. Eekelaar and S. N. Katz (eds), *The Resolution of Family Conflict*, Butterworths, Toronto.

Pearson, J., Thoennes, N. and Vanderkooi, L. (1982) The decision to mediate: profiles of individuals who accept and who reject the opportunity to mediate contested child custody and visitation issues, VI *J. Divorce* 17 (Fall–Winter).

Pruitt, D. G. and Johnson, D. F. (1970) Mediation as an aid to face-saving in negotiation, *Journal of Personality and Social Psychology*, Vol. 14, pp. 239–46.

Roberts, S. (1979) *Order and Dispute*, Penguin, Harmondsworth.

Roberts, S. (1983) Mediation in family disputes, *Modern Law Review*, Vol. 46, no. 5.

Robinson, M. and Parkinson, L. (1985) A family systems approach to conciliation in separation and divorce, *The Journal of Family Therapy*, Vol. 7, pp. 357–77.

Rose, P. (1984) *Parallel Lives*, Penguin, Harmondsworth.

Ross, J. (1986) The Scottish scene: a Summary of recent developments in conciliation throughout Scotland, *Mediation Quarterly*, no. 11.

Rubin, J. Z. and Brown, B. R. (1975) *The Social Psychology of Bargaining and Negotiation*, Academic Press, New York.

Shepherd, G., Howard, J. and Tonkinson, J. (1984) Conciliation: taking it seriously?, *Probation Journal*, Vol. 31, no. 1.

Silbey, S. S. and Merry, S. E. (1986) Mediator settlement strategies, *Law and Policy*, Vol. 8, no. 1.

Smart, C. (1984) *The Ties that Bind*, Routledge & Kegan Paul, London.

Walczak, Y. with Burns, S. (1984) *Divorce: The Child's Point of View*, Harper & Row, London.

Wallerstein, J. and Kelly, J. B. (1980) *Surviving the Break-Up*, Grant McIntyre.

Walrond-Skinner, S. (1976), *Family Therapy: The Treatment of Natural Systems*, Routledge & Kegan Paul, London.

Wegelin, M. M. (1984) *The Policing of Motherhood and Fatherhood after Divorce in the Netherlands*, University of Amsterdam, Grote Bickersstraat 72, 1013 KS Amsterdam.

Index